AUSTRALIAN FOOD

BILL GRANGER

AUSTRALIAN FOOD

BILL GRANGER

murdoch books

Sydney | London

For Natalie.
Her name might not be above the door,
but the door would never open without her.

I would like to pay my respects to the
Gadigal people of the Eora Nation, the traditional custodians
of the land on which our Sydney restaurants stand.

Contents

Every city has one café that becomes the poster child for its inner spirit, and for Sydney, it is bills. Bill had a way of synthesising market produce + eggs + sunshine + freshness into something you didn't know you wanted, but you wanted it bad. Somehow, Bill takes the sunshine with him. The key to Bill's global success is that he changes constantly, and yet has never changed. The principles remain the same — take something people love to eat, and make it fresher, lighter, more beautiful. It's irresistible. It's the sort of food you eat when you're on holidays, and yet you can eat it every day.

Terry Durack, 2009

Sliding Doors theory — in one universe you turn left; in another you hook right. If the theory is true, a world exists where a 23-year-old Bill Granger stays in art school and never opens a café in a remodelled Darlinghurst pub. What a grey world to live in. A universe, potentially, without communal restaurant tables and avocado toast. One in which Granger's ricotta hotcakes don't become Sydney's most iconic dish and the self-taught cook never perfects his recipe for golden, curdy scrambled eggs. Brunch never takes off as A Thing and corn fritters don't become a corpse-reviving constant of every suburban café. Thank heavens that in our universe Granger is better with pans than paints.

Callan Boys, *The Sydney Morning Herald*, 2019

Such defiantly unpretentious food made bills feel like an extension of home and launched a whole new culture of eating in Australia … his uniquely Aussie take on informal dining has been oft-imitated and exported around the globe.

David Prior, *Condé Nast Traveler*, 2016

Bill Granger [is] the restaurateur who is most responsible for the Australian café's global reach.

Amelia Lester, *The New Yorker*, 2018

New Yorkers have taken to the modern breakfasts served at the city's rapidly multiplying Australian cafés ... Mr. Granger had no intention of reinventing the image of Australian food as seen from abroad, but he did.

Julia Moskin, *The New York Times*, 2018

The avocado-on-toast mania can be traced back to one man: Bill Granger, who began serving the now staple brunch dish in 1993.

Milanda Rout, *The Australian WISH* magazine, 2018

You may consider your own scramble the paragon. Or your mother's. Or Julia Child's or Michel Guérard's, served in an eggshell with a jaunty black cap of beluga. Fair enough. But believe me, I would stack Mr. Granger's up against all comers, fully confident that they would hold their own.

RW Apple Jnr, *The New York Times*, 2002

Among Granger's greatest offerings is his reinterpretation of what breakfast should be in a country where breakfast has, until relatively recently, meant a full English, with sausage and bacon and eggs, plus mediocre coffee.

Hannah Goldfield, *T Magazine*, 2015

Renowned as the 'King of breakfast', Granger has always been ahead of the game in terms of food trends. Today, he is celebrated for having brought relaxed, joyful food with a 'sunny twist' to Britain.

Francesca Ryan, *The Telegraph Magazine*, 2016

Introduction

We have a peculiar Australian phrase: 'He's got tickets on himself.'
It's been around for a hundred years, apparently. Australians are a
self-deprecating and modest bunch and we like to chuck this phrase
at anyone who's getting a bit above themselves. I can hear you
wondering, how might you use that in a sentence?

Perhaps something like this: 'That bloke thinks he invented
avocado toast. He's got tickets on himself.'

Another?

'Apparently, this guy knows everything there is to know about
Australian food. He's got tickets on himself.'

What even is Australian food? Healthy, hip and possibly with
a smashed avocado on top? It is true that since I opened bills
Darlinghurst in Sydney in 1993, a joyfully casual sort of Australian
food has backpacked its way across the world, being welcomed
wherever and bringing a touch of Sydney sunshine to restaurant
countertops from New York to Tokyo, Rome to Seoul.

This adoration all feels very new – Australia was long an underdog
in global culinary rankings. When I was growing up, we went quietly
unnoticed beyond our sandstone shores and isolating oceans. I
imagine for anyone outside Australia who bothered to think about
it, our cooking was generally considered to be like British food –
only worse.

However, because of some lucky stars and gratifying quirks of fate,
the world seems to have embraced the Aussie way of eating and fallen
in love with the all-day café. The word that gets used most is 'sunny'.
I love that, but I'm not about to get any tickets on myself.

I have always believed Australia serves the sort of food that brings
people together – over coffee, over communal tables, over all-day
menus – and makes us all feel good. And I don't think it's just the
food – it's the way we eat and serve it. There's always been a casualness
about Australian eating. We've never dressed for dinner (most of
us barely ever use a tablecloth). The majority of us are sprinkled in
towns and cities around the coast of this great wide land, our climate
means we get to eat outside a lot of the time, and we don't need to
be wealthy to enjoy a family picnic by the beach or a barbecue in a
park with friends.

Other than our First Nations peoples, who have their own unique relationship with this land and the traditional food it offers them, we are a population of immigrants who sailed over or blew in from many countries over the past couple of centuries. Australia is often described as a 'melting pot' – which is a glorious culinary term. One in four of us was born overseas; around half have at least one parent from overseas. Sport might be Australia's god, but food is our means of inclusivity. We love food from everywhere. When we sit down to eat we are optimistic and multicultural, without fear or distrust of 'otherness', confident that everyone will bring and share the best of their cuisine to add to the melting pot.

There is no 'set menu' for Australia. Perhaps that's why it's interesting. We're up for anything and open to change. We thrive on sushi one day, pasta the next, fish and chips by the sea, octopus marinated in the Greek style, yum cha on Sunday mornings; our beef might be in a Thai salad or a Vietnamese pho; our chicken could be cooked in an Afghani pulao or Nepalese momo. Australians take pride and excitement in discovering new foods; as a teenager in Melbourne I trekked across town with my friends for the thrill of eating 'the best' Lebanese kofta or African curry. How I love the episode in Nigel Slater's memoir, *Toast*, when his family, as one, distrustfully scrape away their plates of 'foreign' spaghetti and uncomfortably smelly parmesan. In Melbourne we would've walked miles to find the Italian cheese shop selling the most pungent Parmigiano.

So many of our immigrants arrive here and share their food as a way of showing friendship and community. Growing up, my best friend's family had come from China; they started their own restaurant and introduced me to the thrill of dim sum when I was seven. Cha siu bao (barbecued pork bun) was the most amazing thing I'd ever eaten, but, as well as the taste, what I also noticed and stored up in my boyhood brain about food was the atmosphere of joy it could produce – the way a great meal could bring and bind people together.

Being asked to write a book about Australian food, 27 years since the first bills opened, and 20 years after the publication of my first book, *Sydney Food*, has made me take time to think about what were those magical elements that clicked all those years ago in a tiny, sunny, Sydney cornerstore. And, in choosing the 100-odd recipes to feature in this book, how my own particular menu of 'Australian food' came about, and then evolved.

And I still stand by what I said about this when I was asked in 2002: the best restaurants in the world have a strong sense of place. They belong where they are. I just happened to bring the right thing to the right corner.

———

I never really had a plan. Helpful people tried to make me write a 10-year plan, then a 5-year plan. Anyone who knows me knows that a 2-week plan would be ambitious. But I had a hunger to prove myself and make my mark. It was 1993, and until that point I hadn't been able to finish anything. It had taken me three attempts to graduate high school. I'd started architecture at university in Melbourne and left after four months. It says something that I couldn't even finish art school in Sydney — I took off to Tokyo to live for six months, then got distracted and went backpacking around India. But when I decided to open the restaurant I found my groove; I found my tribe.

I had no formal training as a chef and I've always said that, ironically, this was a great training. I wasn't tied down by any rules about food and fine dining. I didn't even know the rules I wasn't supposed to be breaking. It puts me on a parallel with the Australian way of eating: joyfully lacking in fixed assumptions or strict culinary history.

I found a cheap corner site in Darlinghurst (described, fabulously, in one newspaper review at the time as a 'slightly raffish neighbourhood') with a rent I could afford. In fact, it was the only property anyone would allow me to rent. There were a few drawbacks: the local council told me I could only open 7am to 4pm Monday to Saturday, the restaurant was restricted to just 32 seats, and it was the height of a recession. I had no spare cash to splash on interiors. Fortunately, as an ex art student, I had a bit of a feel for design. I liked minimalism, and it was cheap. So was breakfast.

I didn't have a liquor licence — and I had bugger-all chance of getting one — so I had to serve something else to drink. I look back and realise this was one of the easiest decisions of my career: coffee was the nectar of our Melbourne gods. There was nowhere in Sydney you could get good coffee in those days, so I shipped it in from my home town and made fresh juices and smoothies, too.

I wanted bills to feel bright and beachy. Coming from Melbourne, I had quickly grown to love the rhythms of Sydney life: getting up with the sun, wandering down to the ocean and enjoying the outdoors.

I put in a big communal table for people to sit around and fill the space with those seating restrictions. There was no room for big fridges, so we had to bring in fresh ingredients every morning and have no leftovers. We couldn't take credit cards – I didn't know how to set up the system. We couldn't take bookings, either – we didn't have time to answer the phone. And I didn't really cook much except scrambled eggs. What could go wrong?

The art student in me knew I wanted the food to look a certain way – fresh, colourful and not too fiddled around with. We had boxes of ripe tropical fruit delivered and we carefully cut and arranged it to order in bright, eye-catching 'fruit plates'. I knew we wouldn't have a huge menu, but what we did cook would have to be top-notch and produce-driven, to match the coffee. I had the scrambled eggs, plus corn fritters and a recipe for hotcakes I'd adapted from an old Californian cookbook: I changed their cottage cheese to ricotta and made a honeycomb butter instead of the usual maple syrup.

The very casualness of the food seemed to make bills feel like an extension of people's homes. We were simply aiming to be a cheery no-frills breakfast joint with a great atmosphere, smiling service and top breakfasts and coffee. To me, this still sums up everything I think Australian food should say: you don't need wealth and a history of fine dining to enjoy great flavours and a meal in the sun.

Somehow our little café took on a life of its own and summed up the Sydney buzz of the time. The Olympics arrived in town and the world was watching us. Queues formed outside. And along the way, those eggs, corn fritters and hotcakes, the coffee and fresh juices, and that big communal table, somehow launched a whole new culture of eating in Australia. The café started to rival the pub as a place to hang out in during the day and served as proof that daytime eating could be taken just as seriously as night-time dining. The all-day breakfast became a thing. Our café, all cafés, became a 'destination'.

And that avocado? It was just something I always ate. It's true that I put it on toast – but didn't everyone do that? It was just a quick, healthy breakfast on the run. We didn't even sell that much of it. When I was asked to write my first cookbook, I clearly remember thinking: this is ridiculous, putting a recipe for avocado on toast in a book.

———

After two years in Darlinghurst, I was given the chance to open another bills in Sydney's (even-more-raffish-in-those-days) Surry Hills. I'm not naturally a night-time person, but now we had to come up with a dinner menu. I've always liked food that's fresh and light; food that gives us energy rather than absorbing it, even in the evening. My natural inclination was to take the classic comfort food I loved to eat — those homely dishes from the Melbourne 'melting pot' of my boyhood — and update, modernise, tweak them into something a little lighter and fresher. That made sense to me, with our local ingredients and way of living. So we caramelised fresh fruit into compotes instead of heavy sauces, and served crisp, tangy salads in place of the enthusiastically boiled vegetables of my youth. The schnitzel and mash from those early days is still on the menu; the prawn and chilli linguine too, and the roast duck that we served with sticky summer cherries rather than the traditional orange slices.

When we were given the opportunity to open overseas – in Japan, London, Korea, Hawaii (I only open restaurants in places where I already love the food!), that menu was always our starting point. It was our attempt to take a bit of Australian sunshine (and great coffee) wherever we went. Having had so many years to think about it, I think this unpretentious, homely atmosphere is one of the things people enjoy. You can sit in bills in Seoul or Tokyo, or Notting Hill or Darlinghurst, and feel at home in that city, as if you've dropped into a life. For a while you have a window on the world, to drink your coffee and watch it going by.

And the menu also changed, of course, because we'd research the local palate, adding flavours and dishes to fit the sense of place. And then, in turn, we brought those new-favourite flavours home and added them to our Australian melting pot, so we can all enjoy yuzu curd on our breakfast loaf in Darlinghurst, dumplings filled with ricotta and kimchi in Surry Hills and raw tuna poke bowl in Bondi. In the kitchens now we are lucky enough to have chefs from everywhere, all bringing their knowledge and learning together. All of them share the same passion for looking after people.

And, if you ever suspect I might be getting tickets on myself, remember that for every article that puffs me up as the creator of avocado toast, or cook of the 'best scrambled eggs in the world', I'm also the father of teenage girls. Nothing brings you back down to earth quicker than the brutal eye-rolling honesty of your children: 'Avocado on toast? Right, Dad. It's not as if you invented penicillin.'

Classics

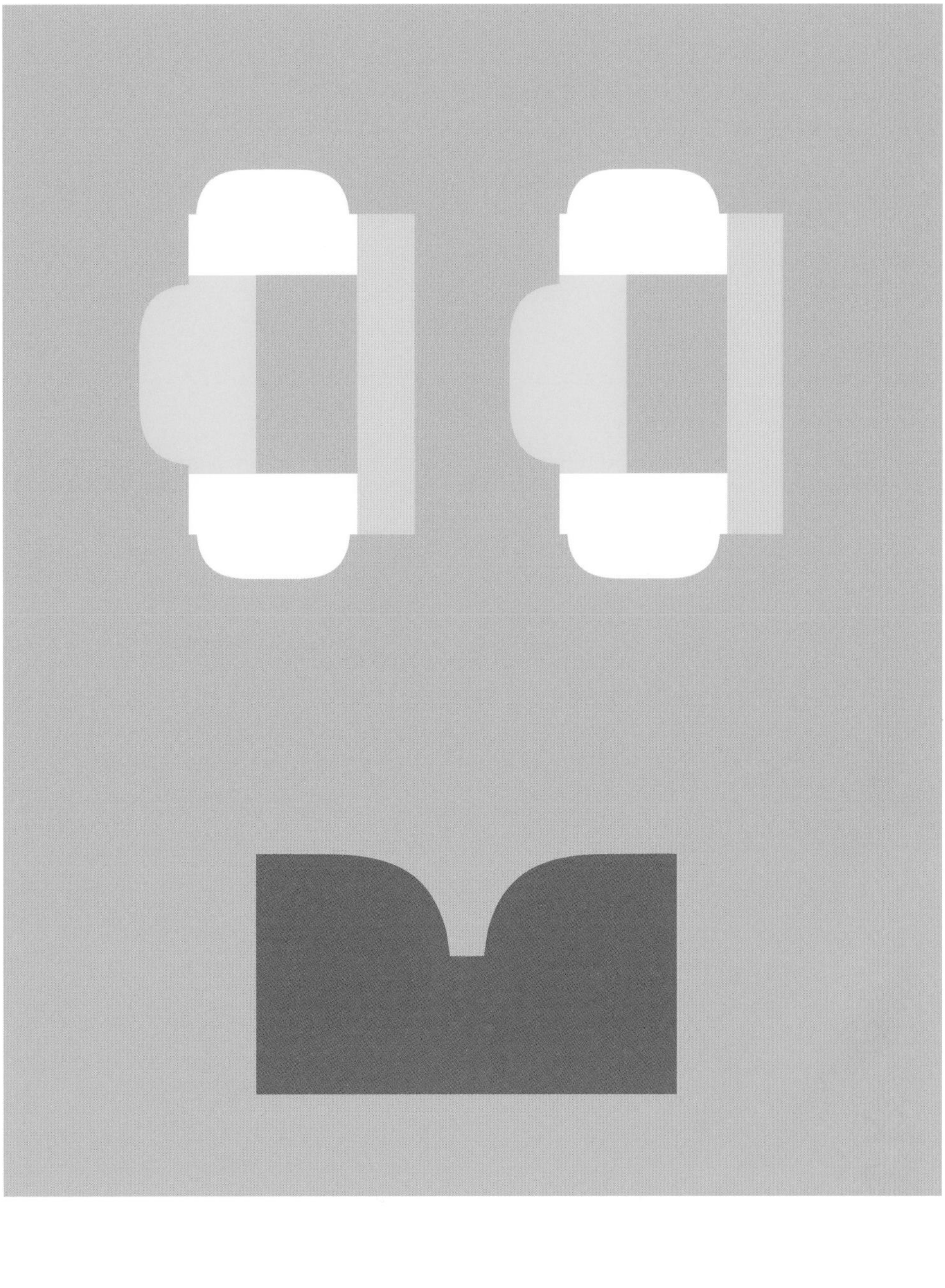

Avocado & poached egg on rye

Serves 4

4 eggs
4 slices rye bread
2 avocados
2 pinches chilli flakes or 1 green chilli, finely sliced
½ small red onion, finely sliced, soaked in cold water, optional
1 large handful coriander leaves
Extra virgin olive oil, to drizzle
1 lime, cut into wedges

Which 'team avo' are you on — sliced, smashed or diced? We serve sliced in the restaurants but at home I usually dice it into a salsa. I've included both options here to avoid a diplomatic incident.

A few newspapers have flatteringly described me as the 'inventor of avocado toast'. Fake news? I suspect it might be, but who would turn down such an accolade?

To poach the eggs, bring 5cm of water to the boil in a frying pan. Turn off the heat and immediately add the eggs. To minimise spreading, break the egg directly into the water, opening the two halves of the shell at the water surface so the egg slides into the water. Cover with a tight-fitting lid and leave undisturbed for about 3 minutes. The eggs are cooked when the whites are opaque. Remove from the pan with a slotted spoon and drain on kitchen paper.

Meanwhile, toast the rye bread. Either arrange slices of avocado on the toast, mash the avocado with a fork on the toast, or dice the avocado and mix with the chilli, red onion and coriander to make a salsa, and arrange on the toast.

Top with a poached egg and scatter with coriander and chilli, if you didn't use them to make a salsa. Season with sea salt, drizzle with olive oil and serve with lime wedges.

Ricotta hotcakes with honeycomb butter & banana

Serves 6–8

Honeycomb

Light-flavoured oil, for greasing
150g caster sugar
75g golden syrup
1½ teaspoons bicarbonate of soda

Honeycomb butter

250g unsalted butter, softened
2 tablespoons runny honey
**90g honeycomb, above or
shop-bought, crushed**

Ricotta hotcakes

300g ricotta
175ml milk
4 eggs, separated
125g plain flour
1 teaspoon baking powder
50g butter

To serve

Icing sugar
**1 banana, halved and sliced
lengthways**

This is the original fluffy ricotta hotcake, on the menu at the first bills, on the first day. In Japan these were credited as the start of the trend for the cloud-like soufflé pancakes described as fluffy or fuwa fuwa – surely the world's best onomatopoeia? Our Japanese kitchen teams have turned them into an art form and now we get letters from people wanting to train as dedicated 'hotcake chefs'.

To make honeycomb, lightly oil a 20cm cake tin. Put the sugar and syrup in a heavy-based pan over medium–low heat. Swirl the pan to dissolve the sugar, then stir with a spatula until all dissolved – this might take 10–15 minutes, so be patient and do not let the mixture bubble at this stage. Turn up the heat, use a sugar thermometer if you have one and heat the mixture to 155°C or until a dark amber caramel. Remove from the heat and quickly stir in the bicarbonate of soda until golden and foaming. Be careful not to overstir: you want to retain as much air in the mixture as possible.

Carefully pour into the tin. Leave to harden and cool for about 90 minutes. Break into chunks and crush with a rolling pin. If you are making honeycomb butter, you will need half the amount, so store the rest in an airtight container at room temperature for up to 2 weeks. You can dip it in melted chocolate and sprinkle over ice cream. Or make double the amount of butter and freeze.

To make the honeycomb butter, blend the ingredients in a food processor until smooth. Roll into a log, wrap in greaseproof paper and chill in the fridge for 2 hours.

To make the hotcakes, mix together the ricotta, milk and egg yolks. Sift the flour, baking powder and a pinch of salt into another bowl. Add the ricotta mixture and stir to combine.

Beat the egg whites in a clean dry bowl until stiff peaks form. Fold into the batter in two batches with a large metal spoon.

Melt a little butter in a large non-stick frying pan. Add 2 tablespoons of batter per hotcake, cooking in batches. Cook over low–medium heat for 2 minutes, or until golden underneath. Turn and cook the other side until golden and cooked through. Serve dusted with icing sugar, with sliced banana and honeycomb butter.

The fresh Aussie

Serves 4

8 eggs

50g greens (silverbeet, cavolo nero,
spring greens, kale), cut into short
lengths and blanched

250g gravlax or tea-smoked salmon

1 avocado, cut into wedges

Extra virgin olive oil, to drizzle

Furikake (Japanese nori sesame
topping), to sprinkle

1 lemon, cut into wedges

Cherry tomato salsa

200g cherry tomatoes, halved

50g spring onions, finely sliced

1 handful coriander leaves

2–3 teaspoons olive oil

When we first opened in Notting Hill we always had the 'full Aussie' on the menu — which is really just a take on the 'full English'. The fresh Aussie is definitely our own. It's a high-protein, low-carb, high-energy big breakfast that keeps you going all day. You can use smoked or tea-smoked salmon here, or any preserved fish.

To poach the eggs, bring 5cm of water to the boil in a frying pan. Turn off the heat and immediately add the eggs. To minimise spreading, break the egg directly into the water, opening the two halves of the shell at the water surface so the egg slides in. Cover with a tight-fitting lid and leave undisturbed for about 3 minutes. The eggs are cooked when the whites are opaque. Remove from the pan with a slotted spoon and drain on kitchen paper.

To make the cherry tomato salsa, mix together all the ingredients.

Arrange the greens, poached eggs, salmon, avocado wedges and cherry tomato salsa on plates. Drizzle the avocado with extra virgin olive oil. Season the avocado and poached eggs with sea salt and freshly ground black pepper and a pinch of furikake. Serve with lemon wedges.

Chocolate banana bread

Makes 8—10 slices

125g unsalted butter, softened

100g caster sugar

4 very ripe bananas, peeled and mashed (about 350g)

2 eggs, lightly beaten

2 teaspoons vanilla extract

250g plain flour

2 teaspoons baking powder

150g dark chocolate, chopped

Banana bread (often a little slice, wrapped in clingfilm) is the quintessential Australian 'pastry' — our home-grown version of the rather-more-sophisticated croissant. This is an update of the recipe published all those years ago in bills Food, *included because, in the early years of the internet when I was excited to google myself (don't ever do that!) this is the recipe that always appeared.*

Palates and tastes change — I've more than halved the sugar and I recommend breaking up a block of good dark chocolate instead of using chocolate chips, which can be overly sweet. If chocolate's not for you in the morning, throw in chopped dates, pecans, walnuts or sultanas instead.

Grease the sides and line the base of a 21 x 10cm loaf tin with baking paper. Preheat the oven to 180°C. Beat together the butter, sugar, banana, eggs and vanilla extract.

Stir together the flour, baking powder and chocolate in a bowl. Gradually stir in the banana mixture, stirring until no flecks of flour are visible.

Pour into the loaf tin and bake for 1 hour, or until a skewer poked into the centre comes out clean.

Leave in the tin to cool for 5 minutes before turning out onto a wire rack. Serve in thick slices spread with butter.

Scrambled eggs

Serves 4

8 eggs
300ml whipping cream
40g butter, plus extra for toast
4 slices sourdough toast
Baby spinach leaves, to serve

Long before I was the 'avocado king', I was apparently the 'egg master'. Early on, The New York Times described the eggs at bills as 'the best scrambled eggs in the world'. We were blown away by such an incredibly great review, but at the time I didn't realise the impact those eggs would have on my life, especially when we were opening in Japan. Can I speak Japanese? No, but I can make scrambled eggs in Japanese on Japanese TV. The texture of food is all-important in Japan — and these have a soft, gentle mouth feel that the TV presenters enthusiastically relished. My dishes are often about the big, fresh, in-your-face flavours Australians love — I like to think the eggs show my gentler, introspective side.

Place the eggs, whipping cream and a good pinch of salt in a large bowl and whisk together.

Melt the butter in a large non-stick frying pan over medium–high heat. Pour in the eggs and leave to cook for 20 seconds, or until gently set around the edge. Gently bring this cooked egg mixture into the centre of the pan; the uncooked egg will naturally flow to the edge of the pan. Continue to gently fold the just-set egg into the centre.

When the eggs are just set, spoon onto buttered toast and serve with a few spinach leaves.

Sweetcorn fritters with roast tomatoes, bacon & avocado salsa

Serves 4

Roast tomatoes

4 ripe Roma tomatoes
4 tablespoons extra virgin olive oil

Avocado salsa

1 large avocado, diced
1½ tomatoes, deseeded and diced
2 tablespoons chopped coriander
2 tablespoons lemon or lime juice
2 tablespoons finely chopped spring onion or red onion
1 dash Tabasco sauce, optional

Sweetcorn fritters

125g plain flour
1 teaspoon baking powder
¼ teaspoon salt
¼ teaspoon paprika
1 tablespoon sugar
2 eggs, lightly beaten
100ml milk
2 corn cobs
½ capsicum (red pepper), diced
2 spring onions, sliced
1 large handful mixed chopped coriander and parsley
4 tablespoons light-flavoured oil, for frying

To serve

Baby spinach or rocket
4 grilled bacon rashers
Extra virgin olive oil, to drizzle

Tex Mex was huge around the time we opened bills. Tinned chipotles were flavour of the month and Navajo blankets were being dragged down every fashionable catwalk. This was in the days before we worried about cultural appropriation, and we were living in a Santa Fe fantasy world. These sweetcorn fritters were my nod to that, but they outlived the phase and are still on the menu. With its combination of crunch and big flavours, this is my own favourite breakfast dish.

To make the roast tomatoes, preheat the oven to 180°C. Place the tomatoes on a baking tray, cut side up, and drizzle with olive oil. Sprinkle liberally with sea salt and freshly ground black pepper. Roast in the oven for 40 minutes.

To make the avocado salsa, gently toss together all the ingredients and season with salt and pepper.

To make the fritters, sift the flour, baking powder, salt and paprika into a large bowl, stir in the sugar and make a well in the centre.

Mix together the eggs and milk and pour slowly into the well in the dry ingredients, whisking to a smooth, lump-free batter. The batter will be quite stiff.

Slice the kernels off the corn cobs and place the corn, capsicum, spring onions and herbs in a mixing bowl. Add just enough batter to lightly bind them. (Any leftover batter can be kept in the fridge for 3 days; do not mix with the corn until you are ready to cook.)

Heat 2 tablespoons oil in a large frying pan over medium heat and drop in 2 tablespoons of batter per fritter, cooking 4 fritters at a time. Cook for 2 minutes, or until the undersides are golden. Turn and cook the other side. Transfer to a plate and keep warm while cooking the rest.

Serve the fritters with roast tomato halves, avocado salsa, a little spinach or rocket and a rasher of bacon. Drizzle with extra virgin olive oil if you like.

Potato & feta fritters with smoked salmon & dill oil

Serves 4

Potato & feta fritters

500g Desiree or other starchy potatoes
1 small onion
2 eggs
2 tablespoons chopped mint
3 tablespoons crumbled feta cheese
3 tablespoons plain flour
4 tablespoons light-flavoured oil,
for frying

Dill oil

50g dill, chopped
100ml olive oil
Zest and juice of ½ lemon

To serve

8 eggs
125g sour cream
1 tablespoon ground sumac
250g smoked salmon or gravlax
1 lemon, cut into wedges

I adore potato rösti. They are my skiing-holiday lunch. I don't ski; I just eat the lunch.

I've been playing around with versions of this recipe for a quarter of a century. I've always been obsessed with potato latkes but I could never write a recipe for them or I'd get all my friends telling me, 'these aren't as good as my mother's'. If you're feeling fancy and own a mandoline (the world's most terrifying kitchen instrument), then use it here to give the potatoes a lovely lacy feel.

Peel and grate the potatoes and onion into a colander, stir in a little salt and leave to drain for 20 minutes. Squeeze out any moisture with your hands.

Beat the eggs lightly and mix with the potatoes and onion. Stir in the mint, feta and flour. Season well with sea salt and freshly ground black pepper.

Heat the oil in a large frying pan. Add 2 tablespoons of fritter mixture to the pan and squash lightly to make a 7cm pancake. Cook 2–3 fritters at a time, depending on the size of your pan (this mixture should make 8–10 fritters). Cook on both sides until golden brown.

To make the dill oil, blend or whisk all the ingredients.

To poach the eggs, bring 5cm of water to the boil in a frying pan. Turn off the heat and immediately add the eggs. To minimise spreading, break the egg directly into the water, opening the two halves of the shell at the surface so the egg slides in. Cover with a tight-fitting lid and leave undisturbed for about 3 minutes. The eggs are cooked when the whites are opaque. Remove from the pan with a slotted spoon and drain on kitchen paper.

Serve the fritters topped with a little sour cream, poached eggs, a sprinkle of sumac and a drizzle of dill oil. Serve with gravlax or salmon and lemon wedges.

Coconut bread

Makes 8–10 thick slices

2 large eggs, lightly beaten
300ml milk
1 teaspoon vanilla extract
375g plain flour, sifted
3 teaspoons baking powder
2 teaspoons ground cinnamon
150g caster sugar
150g shredded or desiccated coconut
75g unsalted butter, melted and cooled

To serve
Unsalted butter
Icing sugar

This foolproof coconut bread is an example of the magpie-like capacities of cooks. We borrow, poach and lend recipes, dropping them like seeds along the way to be picked up and carried by other chefs. When we first opened, I wanted to bake a daily loaf to serve as a variation on the classic banana bread. This recipe came from one of our cooks at the time, who had, in turn, learnt it from a Sri Lankan chef. A very big thank you to both of them.

In the restaurants we serve this in generous thick slices, toasted, buttered and dusted with a little icing sugar. I think there's something about the tropical flavour of coconut that transports us instantly to being 'on holiday'.

Grease the sides and line the base of a 21 x 10cm loaf tin with baking paper. Preheat the oven to 180°C. Mix together the eggs, milk and vanilla.

Stir together the flour, baking powder, cinnamon, sugar and coconut in a large bowl. Make a well in the centre and gradually stir in the egg mixture until just combined. Add the melted butter and stir until just smooth, being careful not to overmix.

Pour into the loaf tin and bake for 1 hour, or until a skewer poked into the centre comes out clean.

Leave in the tin to cool for 5 minutes, then turn out onto a wire rack to cool before slicing. Butter and sprinkle with icing sugar to serve.

Tip

This is easily frozen. Cut into slices first and slip a piece of baking paper between each slice. Store in an airtight container in the freezer and toast straight from frozen.

Seeded breakfast muffins

Makes 12

85ml light-flavoured oil
85ml milk
4 large eggs, lightly beaten
300g plain flour
2½ teaspoons baking powder
½ teaspoon bicarbonate of soda
½ teaspoon ground cinnamon
125g soft brown sugar
25g currants
150g blueberries, raspberries or chopped strawberries
1 large banana, sliced, or 1 apple, grated
1 heaped tablespoon rolled oats
1 heaped tablespoon pepitas (pumpkin seeds)

We always aim to have a fresh-baked muffin on the front counter at bills and Granger & Co. We've been through a few muffin trends, including those huge Texan-style giants with the big muffin tops that became famous on Seinfeld. These small seeded ones are my favourite: they're just the right size, and grainy enough so you don't feel as if you're eating cake for breakfast. And here's a Betty Crocker tip for you — weigh and mix together all the dry ingredients in a bowl, leave it in the fridge, then just stir in the wet ingredients and bake in the morning. Muffins warm from the oven … that's always impressive.

Preheat the oven to 180°C. Line a 12-hole muffin tin with 12 large muffin cases or squares of brown baking paper to form tulip cases.

Mix together the oil, milk and eggs until combined. Put the flour, baking powder, bicarbonate of soda, cinnamon, sugar and currants in a large bowl with a pinch of salt. Pour in the egg mixture and stir to combine.

Gently fold in your chosen fruit — we used raspberries and apple for the photograph.

Spoon into the muffin cases and sprinkle with the oats and pepitas. Bake for 30 minutes, or until a skewer poked into the centre of a muffin comes out clean. Cool on a rack.

Breakfast brioche buns

Makes 12

140ml full-fat milk
20g fresh yeast
50g caster sugar
500g strong white bread flour,
plus extra for dusting
2 teaspoons salt
3 large eggs, lightly beaten
150g softened butter, diced
1 egg, lightly beaten, for glazing
Sesame seeds, optional

Baking your own bread makes all the difference to a breakfast sandwich. I grew up eating bacon and grilled tomato in sliced white. Then we went through the seeded bread phase, and the heady days of the nineties when absolutely everything was served on Turkish, then no bread, and now brioche. I suspect our next craze will be Japanese shokupan milk bread, taking us pretty much full circle.

Heat the milk until just hot but not boiling, then pour into a small bowl. Leave to cool until you can comfortably dip your finger into it, then add the yeast and sugar. Set aside until the yeast has activated and the mixture is foamy.

Put the flour and salt into a mixer fitted with a dough hook. Make a well in the centre and pour in the eggs and yeast mixture. Knead for 15 minutes, or until the dough is smooth, shiny and pulling away from the side of the bowl.

Add the butter to the dough in 3 equal parts, kneading for 2–3 minutes after each addition until there is no sign of any butter. Knead for 15 minutes, until smooth, elastic and glossy. Transfer the dough to a large lightly oiled bowl, cover with oiled plastic wrap and leave in the fridge overnight.

Tip out the dough onto a lightly floured work surface and knock out any air. Fold the dough over on itself 4 times. Divide the dough into 12 portions and shape into balls. Transfer to 2 or 3 lined baking trays, cover loosely with oiled plastic wrap and leave in a warm spot for 1 hour, or until doubled in size.

Preheat the oven to 200°C. Place a deep roasting tin in the bottom of the oven and have a jug of cold water ready. Brush each bun with egg and coat with sesame seeds, if using.

Put the trays of buns into the oven and quickly pour the water into the roasting tin, closing the oven immediately to capture the steam. Bake for 12–15 minutes until the buns are golden, risen and sound hollow when tapped on the base. Cool completely on a wire rack. Fill with bacon, eggs, haloumi, rocket… whatever you fancy.

Grains, Seeds & Juices

Bircher muesli with plum & pomegranate compote

Serves 4

Bircher muesli

125g rolled oats
250g yoghurt
200ml apple juice

Plum & pomegranate compote

300g plums, pitted and quartered
80g caster sugar
3 tablespoons tamarind paste
1 teaspoon vanilla bean paste
100g pomegranate seeds

To serve

4 tablespoons Greek yoghurt

We have tried to take this off the menu a few times over the years but, trust me, we learnt that you don't want to disrupt the Bircher-lover in their morning routine. No one likes to see muesli rage. I love this chilled from the fridge in the Australian summer. It gives off a very Swiss-mountain wholesome vibe.

Stir together the oats, yoghurt, apple juice and 100ml water in a bowl or airtight container. Cover and leave in the fridge overnight.

To make the compote, put the plums, sugar, tamarind and vanilla with 50ml water in a saucepan over medium–high heat. Bring to the boil, then reduce the heat and simmer for 6–8 minutes until the plums are soft but still holding their shape and the juices are syrupy. Leave to cool, then fold in the pomegranate seeds.

Spoon the muesli into bowls and top with a generous helping of compote and a spoonful of Greek yoghurt.

Tip

Any extra compote can be stored in the fridge for up to a week – it is delicious folded through whipped cream and served with meringue as a dessert.

Banana, blueberry & chia seed breakfast bowl

Serves 4

60g chia seeds
150ml coconut water
150ml unsweetened almond milk
300g coconut yoghurt
3 bananas, cut into chunks
200g blueberries
50g pecans or almonds, sliced
Maple syrup, to serve

Does the world really need nourishing with another chia pot? Is it possible we've reached peak wellness? Both valid points, but I just couldn't leave out this recipe — it's such a popular and deliciously effortless modern breakfast to put together for the family. I use almond or oat milk with this — perfect if you're not a big fan of dairy, as one of my daughters isn't. (So much so that her idea of hell is a cheese room.)

Place the chia seeds in a bowl. Add the coconut water, almond milk and a pinch of salt. Leave to soak overnight.

Fold in the coconut yoghurt and spoon into bowls.

Scatter with the bananas, blueberries and nuts, and drizzle with a little maple syrup, to taste.

Sunrise

Serves 2

1 small banana, chopped
2 heaped tablespoons Greek yoghurt
100g frozen berries
200ml apple juice
180ml orange juice
2½ teaspoons runny honey

Blend all ingredients until smooth and pour into 2 glasses. Can be stored in the fridge for 2–3 days; stir before serving.

Espresso & avocado frappé

Serves 2

½ avocado
4 espresso shots (about 80ml)
200g vanilla ice cream
2 cupfuls ice cubes

Scoop the avocado flesh into a strong blender and add the remaining ingredients. Blend to a smooth, thick, slushy consistency. Pour into 2 glasses and serve with spoons.

Honeycomb shake

Serves 2

1 frozen banana, chopped
150g ricotta
80ml milk
2 tablespoons maple syrup
1 cupful ice cubes
20g honeycomb (page 20), crushed, or 2 tablespoons runny honey
Extra honeycomb or honey, optional, to serve

Blend all ingredients until smooth. Pour into 2 glasses and sprinkle with extra honeycomb or drizzle with honey, if you like.

Tip

You can buy honeycomb in the baking section of supermarkets. If you have made your own from the recipe on page 20, you will need 2 matchbox-sized pieces for this.

Bill's raw juice

Serves 2

Raw mix

100g raw cacao powder (or unsweetened cocoa)
100g LSA (ground linseeds, sunflower seeds and almonds)
60g maca powder

1 frozen banana, chopped
2 teaspoons black chia seeds
500ml unsweetened almond milk
2 tablespoons runny honey
1 large handful unskinned almonds or 2 tablespoons almond butter

Combine the raw mix ingredients. This can be stored in an airtight container for up to 3 months.

Blend 1½ tablespoons raw mix with the remaining ingredients until smooth. Pour into 2 glasses and serve – the chia seeds will continue to thicken on standing.

Clockwise from top left: Honeycomb shake; Espresso & avocado frappé; Sunrise; Bill's raw juice

Brown rice & sweet miso porridge with coconut yoghurt & mango

Serves 4

500g cooked brown rice
350ml soy, oat or full-fat milk
2 cardamom pods, seeds removed and ground to a powder
100g sweet white miso paste

To serve

8 tablespoons coconut yoghurt
1 large mango, chopped
4 tablespoons toasted coconut flakes
1 lime, cut into wedges

This is possibly the most delicious way you'll ever find to use up cooked brown rice. Coconut yoghurt is rich and gorgeous and quite unlike regular yoghurt, and this dish was pretty much built around it. You might think the miso sounds an odd addition but it disappears into the porridge and tempers the flavour. Its umami saltiness is what I love. Salt and porridge is a great combination: just ask any Scot.

Put the brown rice, milk and ground cardamom in a saucepan over medium heat and stir until warmed through. Stir in the miso and cook for a further 20 seconds.

Spoon the porridge into bowls and top with a couple of tablespoons of coconut yoghurt, chopped mango and a sprinkling of toasted coconut flakes. Serve with lime wedges.

Granola with blueberry & hibiscus compote

Makes 1.6kg (about 16 portions)

300g rolled oats
250g almonds, roughly chopped
125g sesame seeds
125g blanched hazelnuts, chopped
125g pistachios, chopped
100g pecans, chopped
100g walnuts, chopped
85g sunflower seeds
4 tablespoons desiccated coconut
1½ tablespoons ground cinnamon
1½ teaspoons ground ginger
½ teaspoon salt
125ml apple juice
4 tablespoons light-flavoured oil
5 tablespoons golden syrup
5 tablespoons maple syrup
80g soft brown sugar
200g dried cranberries
125g sultanas

Blueberry & hibiscus compote

2 heaped tablespoons dried hibiscus
flowers (or 6 hibiscus teabags)
300g frozen blueberries
100g sugar

Food is fashion. Some fashions come and go, but others strike a chord and change how we eat forever. Plant-based eating is only growing, which feels like a good thing for all of us — and the planet. This vegan granola will keep everyone happy, with enough servings to keep in an airtight tin for a month of breakfasts. I once tried making this without any sugar, but I missed the lovely crunchy clumpiness it adds. However, you can leave it out if you prefer. Fresh blueberries will send you broke in Australia; fortunately, frozen berries work a treat here. If you don't have hibiscus for the compote, you can use cranberry juice at a pinch.

Preheat the oven to 180°C. Oil 3 large non-stick baking trays.

Mix together the oats, almonds, sesame seeds, hazelnuts, pistachios, pecans, walnuts, sunflower seeds and coconut in a large bowl. Stir in the cinnamon, ginger and salt.

Put the apple juice, oil, syrups and sugar in a pan and heat gently, stirring until the sugar has dissolved and the mixture is liquid. Pour over the dry ingredients and stir to coat well.

Divide between the trays and spread in an even layer. Bake for 25 minutes, stirring every 8 minutes, until the granola is light golden brown and toasted. Leave to cool on the trays. Pour into a large bowl and stir in the dried fruit.

To make the compote, put the hibiscus in a pan with 100ml water and slowly bring to the boil. Remove from the heat and leave for 5 minutes until the water is deep pink. Strain the liquid through a sieve, discarding the hibiscus.

Put the strained liquid back into the pan on the heat and add the blueberries and sugar. Stir to dissolve the sugar, then simmer for 8–10 minutes until syrupy. The compote can be stored, covered, in the fridge for up to 1 week.

Tip

Granola can be stored in a tin for a month — you can also use it as crumble topping or eat it as a snack, like trail mix.

Quinoa & oat porridge with sweet red bean, apple & almond butter

Serves 4

50g buckwheat or millet
50g quinoa
125g rolled oats
300ml unsweetened almond milk
120g red bean paste
4 tablespoons almond butter
1 green apple, cut into matchsticks
4 tablespoons toasted flaked almonds

When I was living in Japan when I was 19, I visited the famous Andersen Bakery. There, piled high, were the most incredible looking doughnuts. After months of Japanese food I was craving sweet, doughy carbs. What I hadn't realised, as I bit in, was that the doughnut was flavoured with red bean paste, beloved in Japanese desserts. My taste buds were expecting Aussie tuck-shop jam, and this sure was a surprise. How times change. I'm now very partial to a traditional red bean sweet dish. If you haven't tried it, do give it a go — I imagine you'll be more open-minded than my 19-year-old self.

Place the buckwheat or millet and quinoa in a small saucepan with 300ml water and bring to the boil over high heat. Reduce the heat and simmer for 15 minutes, or until just tender and the water has been absorbed — you might need to top up with more boiling water during cooking. Remove from the heat and set aside.

Meanwhile, put the oats, almond milk and 300ml water in a saucepan over medium heat. Bring to the boil, stirring continuously, then simmer for 3 minutes, until the porridge is thick and creamy.

Add the cooked buckwheat or millet and quinoa to the porridge, stir in the red bean paste and heat through. Add a splash more milk if the mixture is too thick.

Spoon the porridge into bowls, top with almond butter, apple and flaked almonds and serve immediately.

Bill's green juice

Serves 2

1 tablespoon chia seeds
80ml coconut water
1 large cucumber, roughly chopped
4 large handfuls silverbeet or spinach leaves,
tough stalks discarded
4 green apples, cored and quartered
4 celery stalks
5cm piece fresh ginger, peeled

Put the chia seeds and coconut water in a
small bowl and leave for 10 minutes, stirring
occasionally until the chia has swelled up.

Put the cucumber, silverbeet, apple, celery and
ginger through a juicer. Pour the chia mix into
2 glasses and top up with the green vegetable
juice. Serve immediately – the chia seeds will
continue to thicken on standing.

Mango passionfruit frappé

Serves 2

300g frozen mango flesh
Pulp of 4 ripe passionfruit
2½ tablespoons agave syrup or runny honey
Juice of 1 small lime
1 cupful ice cubes

Place all the ingredients into a strong blender
with 200ml water. Blend until smooth, thick and
slushy. Pour into 2 glasses and serve with spoons.

Pineapple, turmeric & coconut juice

Serves 2

1 pineapple, peeled and roughly chopped
2 apples, cored and quartered
80g fresh turmeric, roughly peeled if necessary
60ml coconut water

Put the pineapple, apple and turmeric through
a juicer. Pour into 2 glasses and top up with
coconut water to serve.

Raspberry shiso frappé

Serves 2

120g frozen raspberries or other berries
Juice of 1 lemon
50ml cranberry juice
3 tablespoons agave syrup or runny honey
2 shiso leaves
1 cupful ice cubes

Put all the ingredients into a strong blender
with 150ml water. Blend until smooth, thick and
slushy. Pour into 2 glasses and serve with spoons.

Clockwise from top left: Bill's green juice;
Mango passionfruit frappé; Raspberry shiso frappé;
Pineapple, turmeric & coconut juice

Coconut rice pudding with red papaya, raspberry & pistachio

Serves 4

Coconut rice pudding

150g short-grain pudding rice
400ml coconut milk
50g caster sugar
2½ teaspoons vanilla bean paste

Red papaya purée

½ red papaya, peeled and chopped
(around 150g papaya flesh)
5 teaspoons orange juice
2 teaspoons maple syrup

To serve

½ red papaya, peeled and diced
1 large handful raspberries
1 handful toasted pistachios, chopped

Pudding for breakfast? I am a child of the seventies, when rice pudding was the only dessert we ever ate at home. My mum made it in the traditional English way — rice, sugar, milk and a sprinkle of nutmeg, baked in the oven. That nutmeggy skin was definitely a love/hate element (sadly, I was in the second camp). I can't believe it's taken us around 200 years to revise rice pudding into something rather more suited to the Australian climate. Chilled coconut rice pudding for breakfast is a perfect example of traditional English fare updated for the modern Australian palate.

To make the rice pudding, put the rice, coconut milk, sugar, vanilla and 300ml water in a saucepan. Bring to the boil over high heat, then reduce to simmer for 30–40 minutes, until the rice is soft, adding a little more boiling water if it ever looks dry. Remove from the heat and spread on a baking tray to cool.

Meanwhile, to make the papaya purée, mix the ingredients in a blender until smooth.

Spoon the rice pudding into bowls and top with the papaya purée, diced papaya and raspberries. Sprinkle with toasted pistachios to serve.

Tip

Any left-over rice pudding and papaya purée can be stored in the fridge for up to 2 days.

Buckwheat bowl with sprouting seeds & rose harissa

Serves 4

85g buckwheat
50g mixed quinoa
Olive oil
4 eggs
200g Greek yoghurt
2 avocados, chopped
2 small beetroot, cut into matchsticks
1 tablespoon mixed sprouted seeds
4 tablespoons rose harissa
1 handful pepitas (pumpkin seeds)
1 handful roasted almonds, chopped
1 handful coriander leaves
1 lime, cut into wedges

All those years ago, when bills first opened, breakfast was most definitely bacon, eggs and pancakes. No matter what people were excited to eat for lunch or dinner, there was no way that any Australian would've countenanced a bowl of buckwheat for breakfast. And you would have been run out of town for suggesting such nonsense. Fast forward 25 years and these healthy breakfast bowls are a staple. I'm thanking Instagram for this — the greasy hangover fry-up doesn't signal virtue in quite the same way.

Cover the buckwheat with 180ml cold water in a small pan and bring to the boil. Reduce the heat and simmer for 8–10 minutes until the buckwheat is tender. Remove from the heat and leave until the grains have absorbed all the water.

Put the quinoa in a pan and cover with 150ml cold water. Bring to the boil, reduce the heat and cook for 12–15 minutes, until the grains are tender and the water has been absorbed.

Tip both grains into a bowl and stir together. Drizzle with olive oil, season well and set aside to cool.

To poach the eggs, bring 5cm of water to the boil in a frying pan. Turn off the heat and immediately add the eggs. To minimise spreading, break the egg directly into the water, opening the two halves of the shell at the surface so the egg slides in. Cover with a tight-fitting lid and leave undisturbed for about 3 minutes. The eggs are cooked when the whites are opaque. Remove from the pan with a slotted spoon and drain on kitchen paper.

Divide the yoghurt between 4 serving plates, spoon on the mixed grains, and add a poached egg, half an avocado and some beetroot. Sprinkle with mixed sprouted seeds, add a tablespoon of rose harissa and finish with pepitas, almonds and coriander leaves. Serve with lime wedges.

Breakfast Plates

Chickpea pancakes with spiced roast cauliflower & carrots

Serves 4

Spiced roast cauliflower & carrots

1 large cauliflower, broken into florets
3 large carrots, cut into chunks
2 tablespoons light-flavoured oil
1 tablespoon black mustard seeds
2 teaspoons cumin seeds
1 teaspoon coriander seeds, cracked
½ teaspoon ground turmeric
½ teaspoon chilli flakes

Chickpea pancakes

150g chickpea flour (gram or besan)
½ teaspoon salt
½ teaspoon ground cumin
2 spring onions, finely sliced
2cm piece fresh ginger, peeled and finely chopped
1 garlic clove, crushed
1 green chilli, deseeded and chopped
1 handful coriander, roughly chopped
2 tablespoons light-flavoured oil, for frying

To serve

Greek yoghurt
1 small red onion, sliced
1 green chilli, finely sliced
1 handful coriander leaves

Chickpea flour is fantastic to have in your cupboard at all times — it needs no egg to hold it together in a batter, so is handy in vegan cooking. This pancake batter can last a couple of days in the fridge.

Why has it taken us until now to fall in love with roast cauliflower? Why did the poor cauliflower have to endure decades of being boiled to mush, with the smell of its torment filling every kitchen? Let us all enjoy its reign as a current superfood.

For the spiced roast vegetables, preheat the oven to 220°C. Place the cauliflower and carrots on a large baking tray where they fit in a single layer. Drizzle with oil and season with salt. Roast for 15 minutes, or until beginning to char. Reduce the oven to 200°C, stir in the spices and chilli flakes and roast for a further 5 minutes.

Meanwhile, for the pancakes, mix the flour, salt and cumin together in a large bowl. Slowly pour in 250ml water, stirring to make a smooth batter. Add the spring onions, ginger, garlic, chilli and coriander. Mix well and set aside for 15 minutes.

Heat a little oil in a frying pan over medium heat. Ladle a quarter of the batter into the pan and tilt to spread evenly. Cook for 3 minutes. Turn over and cook for 2 minutes until golden. Cook the remaining batter to make 4 pancakes.

Spoon the roasted vegetables over the pancakes. Top with yoghurt, red onion, chilli and coriander to serve.

Grilled cheese & kimchi open sandwich

Serves 4

4 slices sourdough bread
4 tablespoons good-quality mayonnaise
1 garlic clove, crushed
200g kimchi
120g cheddar cheese, grated
120g comte cheese, grated
80g mozzarella cheese, grated
1 large handful coriander leaves
2 spring onions, finely sliced
1 red chilli, finely sliced

What a perfect mix of Eastern and Western flavours: bubbling cheese on toast with kimchi is a delicious update of my favourite cheddar and pickle sandwich. The Sydney Morning Herald *has dubbed this the 'new avocado on toast' and I've noticed it popping up on a few menus in London recently, so it feels like a new classic in the making. Bloody brilliant with a Bloody Mary for brunch.*

Heat the grill to medium–high. Lightly toast the sourdough on one side until golden.

Mix the mayonnaise with the garlic. Spread on the untoasted side of the bread, and then top with the kimchi. Mix the cheeses together and sprinkle over the bread, pressing down gently. Grill for 2–3 minutes until melted and golden.

Serve immediately, sprinkled with coriander, spring onion and red chilli.

Tofu scramble with shredded cabbage & chilli sambal on sourdough toast

Serves 4

Chilli sambal

5 red chillies, roughly chopped
4 garlic cloves, roughly chopped
2.5cm piece galangal, peeled and roughly chopped
2.5cm piece fresh ginger, peeled and roughly chopped
1 large French shallot, roughly chopped
3 tablespoons light-flavoured oil
1 tablespoon chilli flakes
60g palm sugar, crumbled or grated
2 teaspoons tamarind paste
1 tablespoon tamari
Juice of ½ lime

Tofu scramble

2 tablespoons light-flavoured oil
2 garlic cloves, crushed
2.5cm piece fresh ginger, peeled and grated
4 spring onions, finely chopped
1½ teaspoons curry powder
1½ teaspoons ground turmeric
1½ teaspoons ground coriander
560g silken tofu

To serve

¼ sweet heart cabbage (or firm white cabbage), shredded
½ cucumber, peeled into ribbons
1 large handful mint leaves
1 large handful coriander leaves
Juice of 1 lime
Olive oil
4 slices sourdough bread
4 tablespoons crispy shallots

It goes without saying that I love scrambled eggs, but these days I seem to be eating scrambled tofu more often. It can be very basic — just scrambled with a little tamari — or a bit more involved, like this dish. I spent so many years cooking scrambled eggs at 6am that I have a recurring nightmare: customers are waiting outside, I've overslept and am now in the kitchen cooking eggs in the nude. I fear this has made me prefer tofu.

For the chilli sambal, mix the chillies, garlic, galangal, ginger and shallot to a paste in a small food processor or mortar and pestle.

Heat the oil in a frying pan over medium heat and fry the paste for 5–8 minutes until dark red and fragrant. Add the chilli flakes and palm sugar and stir to dissolve the sugar. Add the tamarind paste and tamari and cook for a further 2–5 minutes until the sauce is thick. Remove from the heat, add the lime juice and leave to cool. This can be stored in the fridge for up to a month.

To make the tofu scramble, heat the oil in a large non-stick frying pan over medium–high heat. Fry the garlic and ginger for 1 minute, then add the spring onions, curry powder, turmeric and coriander and fry, stirring, for a further minute. Crumble in the silken tofu and stir to coat in the spice mixture — the tofu will look like scrambled eggs.

Toss together the cabbage, cucumber and herbs with the lime juice and a good splash of olive oil. Season well.

Toast the bread under a hot grill until golden. Top each slice of toast with tofu and add a handful of cabbage, cucumber and herbs. Sprinkle with crispy shallots and serve with a generous spoonful of chilli sambal.

Crisp-bottomed rice with fried eggs & pickles

Serves 4

200g brown rice
250ml chicken or vegetable stock
1 tablespoon sesame oil
1 piece dried kombu, optional
125g arame or hijiki seaweed, optional

Spicy sauce

4 tablespoons Korean chilli bean paste (gochujang)
2 tablespoons rice wine vinegar
2 teaspoons runny honey or maple syrup
3 teaspoons sesame oil

Carrot pickles

1 tablespoon rice vinegar
½ teaspoon caster sugar
2 generous pinches salt
1 large carrot, finely sliced (try some heritage varieties)

2 tablespoons light-flavoured oil, plus extra for frying the eggs
4 eggs
Chilli powder or flakes, to taste
1 small cucumber or zucchini (courgette), julienned or grated
½ small red onion, finely sliced, soaked in cold water for 5 minutes, drained
1 handful micro cress

This is a reworking of bibimbap, and started life in our restaurants around 2015. Our chef, Julian, created the restaurant version at peak hipster movement and it was called 'chicken fat rice'. We were on the cusp of dude food and clean eating. With a name like that, not surprisingly, it didn't sell as well as it could have. The 'dude' idea of food drifted and the healthier side came bouncing in. Out went the chicken fat and in came a new vegetarian breakfast star.

If you aren't vegetarian, use chicken stock here; swap it for vegetable stock if you are. And if you have some left-over chicken fat, from skimming the chicken stock, use it here to fry the rice. It does make the dish extra sumptuous.

Put the rice, stock, sesame oil, kombu and 250ml water in a saucepan with a tight-fitting lid. Bring to the boil, reduce the heat to low, cover the pan and cook for 25 minutes. Turn off the heat and leave to stand for a further 10–15 minutes without removing the lid. Remove the kombu and stir in the arame or hijiki seaweed.

Meanwhile, to make the spicy sauce, whisk together all the ingredients in a small bowl. Set aside until ready to serve.

For the carrot pickles, mix together the rice vinegar, caster sugar and salt until dissolved. Add the carrot and toss gently. Set aside until ready to serve.

Heat the oil in a heavy-based pan (something you can serve in – cast iron would be perfect) over medium–high heat. Add the rice and cook for 5 minutes, until the rice is catching on the bottom of the pan but not burning.

Meanwhile, fry the eggs in a little oil in a separate frying pan over medium–high heat. Sprinkle with a little chilli powder or flakes. Remove the rice from the heat, top with the fried eggs, pickles, cucumber or zucchini, onion and micro cress, and serve in the pan with the spicy sauce on the side.

Brunch bowl with green tea noodles, edamame & salmon

Serves 4

Mushroom & wakame dashi

1½ tablespoons dashi
1½ tablespoons dried wakame
1½ teaspoons mirin
3 dried shiitake mushrooms
1½ tablespoons miso paste
3 fresh shiitake mushrooms, finely sliced

Cucumber & carrot pickles

1 tablespoon rice vinegar
½ teaspoon caster sugar
¼ teaspoon salt
1 carrot, peeled into ribbons
½ cucumber, peeled into ribbons

200g green tea, soba or buckwheat noodles or brown rice
2 teaspoons light-flavoured oil
200g edamame beans
2 avocados, halved
4 tablespoons sesame seeds, toasted
4 eggs
2 hot smoked salmon fillets, flaked
1 red chilli, finely sliced
4 spring onions, finely sliced
8 radishes, finely sliced
1 handful shiso leaves

It's oddly difficult to go out for breakfast in Japan. It's a meal the Japanese tend to always eat at home, the exception being the hotel breakfast — and what a beauty that is. It arrives on a perfect tray with all the ingredients — tiny pickles and fish — arranged in tiny dishes, like tiny artworks. This is very much my Australian version of that beautiful concept, but all in one bowl. It's definitely got a temple-food vibe and makes you feel virtuous in its freshness. The Japanese would never serve noodles in this setting, so I'm breaking some kitchen rules.

To make the mushroom & wakame dashi, put the dashi, wakame, mirin, dried shiitakes and 800ml water in a pan. Bring to the boil, then simmer for 5 minutes. Stir in the miso and sliced shiitakes and remove from the heat.

For the cucumber & carrot pickles, mix together the rice vinegar, caster sugar and salt until dissolved. Add the carrot and cucumber and toss gently. Set aside until ready to use.

Meanwhile, cook the noodles according to the packet instructions, drain and cool under cold water. Drain again and drizzle with the oil to stop them sticking.

Cook the edamame in boiling salted water for 4 minutes, then drain well. Coat the avocado halves with sesame seeds.

To poach the eggs, bring 5cm water to the boil in a frying pan. Turn off the heat and add the eggs at once: to minimise spreading, break the egg directly into the water, carefully opening the two halves of the shell at the surface so the egg slides in. Cover with a tight-fitting lid and leave to cook undisturbed for about 3 minutes. The eggs are cooked when the whites are opaque. Remove from the pan with a slotted spoon and drain on kitchen paper.

Divide the noodles between 4 bowls. Pour the dashi over the noodles along with some wakame and shiitake mushrooms. Add the edamame, a poached egg, sesame-coated avocado, flaked salmon, chilli, spring onion, radish and shiso. Serve with cucumber & carrot pickles.

Sugar-cured prawn omelette with salsa rossa

Serves 4

Salsa rossa

1 garlic clove, crushed

1 small red onion, finely chopped

1 red chilli, finely chopped

2 anchovy fillets, finely chopped

2 tablespoons olive oil

1 tablespoon red wine vinegar

2 roasted red capsicums (peppers) in olive oil, drained and finely chopped

2 Roma tomatoes, deseeded and finely chopped

75g caster sugar

2 teaspoons salt

1 lemongrass stalk, white part only, bruised and roughly chopped

250g raw prawns, peeled and deveined

6 eggs, lightly beaten

6 spring onions, finely sliced

2.5 cm piece fresh ginger, peeled and very finely chopped or grated

2 tablespoons sesame oil

1 large handful coriander leaves

Rocket, to serve

1 lime, cut into wedges

This is Australia meets Hawaii on a plate. When we were in the last hectic stages of opening the restaurant in Hawaii, our chef threw this together for staff breakfast with prawns that were in the fridge. We had some salsa rossa that we generally used on pizzas, but what a match it was with those sweet prawns.

To make the salsa rossa, mix all the ingredients together and season with sea salt and freshly ground black pepper. Leftovers can be kept in the fridge for up to 3 days to serve with meat, fish, chicken, or even spooned over pizzas.

Put the sugar, salt and lemongrass in a food processor and mix well. Transfer to a bowl, add the prawns, toss well, cover and leave for 30 minutes.

Transfer the prawns to a sieve, rinse and drain. Pat dry with kitchen paper and cut into bite-sized pieces. Mix the prawns with the eggs, spring onion and ginger to make a batter.

Heat 2 teaspoons oil in a non-stick frying pan over medium heat. Add a quarter of the omelette batter and cook until just set on the bottom and light golden. Turn over and cook for another 1 minute. Slide onto a warmed plate and cook the remaining 3 omelettes.

Serve with coriander, rocket, lime wedges and salsa rossa.

Zucchini fritters with cavolo nero & quinoa

Serves 4

Tahini yoghurt

4 tablespoons tahini
Juice of ½ lemon
1 garlic clove, crushed
100g Greek yoghurt
2 tablespoons olive oil
½ teaspoon nigella seeds, toasted

Cavolo nero & quinoa salad

80g cavolo nero, stalks discarded,
leaves shredded
2 tablespoons olive oil
Juice of ½ lemon
400g cooked quinoa
4 radishes, finely sliced
3 spring onions, finely sliced
1 handful mint, roughly chopped
1 handful coriander, roughly chopped
Ground sumac, to sprinkle

Zucchini fritters

300g (about 2 large) zucchini
(courgettes), coarsely grated
200g potato, coarsely grated
1 teaspoon fine salt
1 small garlic clove, crushed
2 spring onions, finely chopped
3 tablespoons chickpea flour (gram
or besan)

125ml light-flavoured oil, for frying
250g haloumi, cut into 8 slices

Zucchini (courgette) fritters are the 'big vegetarian breakfast' in Australia; they're rich and filling. If you don't want to go to the trouble of cooking the haloumi separately, you can grate it through the fritter mixture.

To make the tahini yoghurt, mix together all the ingredients. Any leftovers can be stored in the fridge for up to 3 days.

To make the cavolo nero & quinoa salad, mix the cavolo nero with the olive oil, lemon juice and a good pinch of salt. Leave for 15 minutes. Add the quinoa, radish and spring onions and toss well. Gently fold in the herbs. Sprinkle with sumac.

To make the zucchini fritters, mix together the zucchini, potato and salt in a sieve over a large bowl and leave to drain for 15 minutes. Use your hands or a clean tea towel to squeeze out the liquid.

Transfer the zucchini mixture to a bowl and add the garlic, spring onion and flour. Toss together well. Divide the mixture into 12 balls, each about the size of a golf ball.

Heat the oil in a deep frying pan over medium–high heat. Fry the fritters, a few at a time so you don't overcrowd the pan, for 3 minutes or until dark golden and crisp, turning once. Remove with a slotted spoon and drain on kitchen paper sprinkled with salt. Keep warm and cook the rest.

When the fritters have all been cooked, fry the haloumi for 1 minute on each side until golden.

Serve the fritters and haloumi with tahini yoghurt and cavolo nero & quinoa salad. Sprinkle with sumac before serving.

Baked green eggs with roast tomato & chilli salsa

Serves 4

Roast tomato & chilli salsa

2 large Roma tomatoes

1 large red chilli

2 tablespoons olive oil

1 teaspoon sweet smoked paprika

500g Swiss chard or silverbeet

4 tablespoons olive oil

3 garlic cloves, finely chopped

2 teaspoons cardamom pods, seeds removed and ground, or ground cardamom

2 teaspoons ground coriander

2 teaspoons cumin seeds

2 teaspoons fennel seeds

200ml double cream

Juice of ½ lemon

8 eggs

4 heaped tablespoons sour cream

Sweet smoked paprika, to sprinkle

Sourdough toast, to serve

Baked eggs are the organised entertainer's dream. (I always think I'm going to be 'the organised entertainer' but I can never quite be that person. If there's ever a chance that I'm being organised, I get over-enthusiastic and add something else into the equation, causing chaos.) What you need here is an oven tray with lots of little baking dishes. You can even fill the dishes and keep them in the fridge overnight, ready to bake the next day.

To make the roast tomato & chilli salsa, using tongs, hold the tomatoes and chilli directly over a gas flame, or cook over a hot barbecue or under a hot grill, for 5–10 minutes, turning frequently until blackened. Remove from the heat and place in an airtight container. Leave for 5 minutes, then peel away the charred skins and any stalks. Halve the tomatoes, discard the seeds and chop the flesh. Finely chop the chilli and add to the tomato with the oil and sweet smoked paprika. Set aside until ready to serve.

Shred the chard leaves and set aside; finely slice the stalks. Heat the oil in a large frying pan over medium heat, add the chard stalks, garlic and spices and cook for 10 minutes, stirring frequently, until the stalks are tender.

Add the shredded leaves to the pan with 2–3 tablespoons water and cook for 5–8 minutes, until the leaves are wilted and soft. Increase the heat, pour in the cream and lemon juice and simmer for 3 minutes to reduce the cream. Season with sea salt and freshly ground black pepper.

Preheat the oven to 200°C. Spoon the chard mixture into four 250–300ml ovenproof dishes. Make 2 holes in the mixture and crack an egg into each hole. Cover with foil and bake for 12–15 minutes, or until the whites are set and the yolks runny.

Add a spoonful of sour cream and roast tomato & chilli salsa to each dish. Sprinkle with smoked paprika and serve with sourdough toast.

Prawn, xo & chorizo fried rice

Serves 4

Pickled cucumber

2 tablespoons rice vinegar
1 teaspoon caster sugar
½ teaspoon salt
½ cucumber, roughly chopped

1 tablespoon light-flavoured oil
1 tablespoon sesame oil
2.5cm piece fresh ginger, peeled and finely chopped
2 garlic cloves, finely chopped
200g chorizo, roughly chopped
16 raw prawns, peeled and deveined
4 spring onions, chopped
2 tablespoons XO sauce
600g cooked short-grain brown rice
2 tablespoons soy sauce
4 eggs
4 tablespoons crispy shallots
1 large handful coriander
1 lime, cut into wedges

For lots of people of my era who grew up in Australia, fried rice is the ultimate comfort food. Prawn and chorizo is real Aussie surf and turf. This is endlessly versatile. Often I stir in a couple of tablespoons of kimchi when I've fried the prawns, and in the restaurant we often swap out the chorizo and add a tablespoon of nduja with the prawns.

To make the pickled cucumber, mix the vinegar, sugar and salt in a bowl, stirring until dissolved. Add the cucumber and toss to coat in the pickling liquid. Set aside.

Heat both oils in a wok over medium–high heat. Add the ginger, garlic and chorizo and stir-fry for 3 minutes until the red oils come out of the chorizo. Add the prawns and spring onion and cook until the prawns are pink. Stir in the XO sauce. Add the cooked rice and soy sauce and stir-fry for 3 minutes until mixed together. Keep warm.

To poach the eggs, bring 5cm water to the boil in a frying pan. Turn off the heat and add the eggs at once. To minimise spreading, break the egg directly into the water, carefully opening the two halves of the shell at the surface so the egg slides in. Cover with a tight-fitting lid and leave undisturbed for about 3 minutes. The eggs are cooked when the whites are opaque. Remove from the pan with a slotted spoon and drain on kitchen paper.

Divide the fried rice between 4 bowls and add a poached egg, crispy shallots, coriander, some pickled cucumber and a lime wedge. Serve immediately.

Tip

Shop-bought crispy shallots and XO sauce can be found at Asian supermarkets. If you can't find XO, use shrimp paste or even a tablespoon of fish sauce, with a tablespoon of chilli sauce for heat.

Bakery

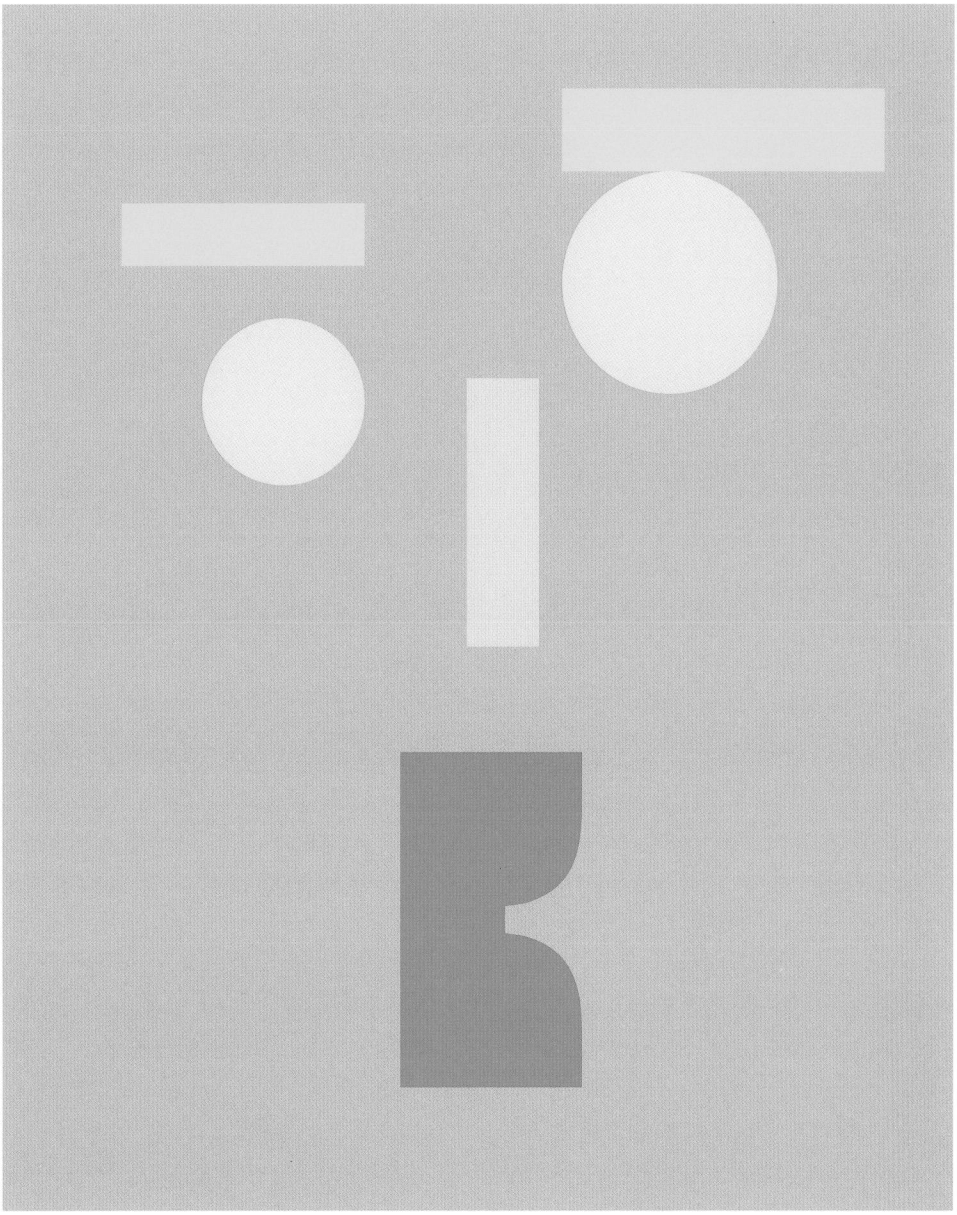

Granola bars

150g gluten-free rolled oats
60g gluten-free flour
2 tablespoons desiccated coconut
½ teaspoon salt
½ teaspoon baking powder
½ teaspoon ground cinnamon
60g sultanas
75g dried cranberries
75g pitted dates, chopped
4 tablespoons mixed sesame seeds
4 tablespoons pepitas (pumpkin seeds)
4 tablespoons sunflower seeds
2 tablespoons linseeds
100g peanut butter
90g honey
100g butter, diced
50g golden syrup
½ teaspoon bicarbonate of soda

I see the old-fashioned granola bar as a wonderful example of Darwin's theory of natural selection … it has survived the no-sugar paleo movement that's been particularly huge in Australia, but has had to adapt and go gluten-free to survive in today's fast-paced food world.

Running a restaurant is a little like hosting a dinner party for 100 guests every day — you want to cater for all tastes and keep everybody happy and well fed. You could use regular flour and oats if you are not sensitive to gluten.

Preheat the oven to 180°C. Lightly grease and line a deep 20 x 25cm baking tray with greaseproof paper.

Stir together the oats, flour, coconut, salt, baking powder and cinnamon in a large bowl. Add the dried fruit and seeds and mix well.

Stir together the peanut butter, honey, butter, syrup and 1 tablespoon water in a small pan over medium heat. Heat until the peanut butter has melted.

Add the bicarbonate of soda to the dry ingredients, then pour in the peanut butter mixture and stir until everything is coated. Scrape into the tin and bake for 25–30 minutes until golden brown.

Cool completely in the tin before turning out and cutting into bars. These will keep in an airtight container for up to a week.

Miso caramel brownies

Makes 16 brownies

Miso caramel

110g sugar
50g unsalted butter, diced
1 tablespoon white miso paste

250g caster sugar
85g cocoa powder, plus extra to serve
55g plain flour
1 teaspoon baking powder
3 large eggs, lightly beaten
200g unsalted butter, melted
2 teaspoons vanilla extract
200g dark chocolate, melted

Why are brownies such a long-standing café favourite? I'll let you in on a trade secret: it's because they're so easy and reliable. Absolutely no skill set is needed to make a completely delicious chocolate brownie.

Miso is definitely an 'it' ingredient of the twenty-first century so far – its umami richness cuts through the sweetness of the caramel and gives this old favourite an extraordinary new twist. Be warned: these are rich. Cut them into the tiniest of squares to serve.

To make the miso caramel, melt the sugar in a non-stick frying pan over medium heat, swirling the pan to help it melt. Once it's dissolved, increase the heat and boil until the sugar is light golden brown. Quickly whisk in the butter, followed by the miso. The caramel should be smooth and rich. Remove from the heat and leave to cool.

Preheat the oven to 180°C. Lightly grease and line a 20cm square baking tin with baking paper.

Stir together the caster sugar, cocoa powder, flour and baking powder in a bowl. Mix together the eggs, melted butter and vanilla, then stir into the dry ingredients until combined. Fold in the melted chocolate.

Pour half the brownie mixture into the tin, pour in the miso caramel and then finish by carefully pouring the rest of the brownie mixture over the top. Smooth the surface. Bake for 30 minutes.

Leave to cool completely in the tin before cutting into small squares and dusting with extra cocoa to serve.

Pumpkin & cardamom breakfast loaf

Makes 15 slices

115g dates, pitted and roughly chopped
1 teaspoon bicarbonate of soda
1 tablespoon chia seeds
235g mashed cooked pumpkin
165g brown sugar
125g coconut yoghurt
220g gluten-free flour
50g desiccated coconut
1 teaspoon baking powder
1 teaspoon ground cinnamon
½ nutmeg, finely grated
1 teaspoon ground cardamom

With this great breakfast loaf you can be best friend to the gluten-free, king of the dairy-free, and beloved of the egg-free. It is a very moist and quite unusual loaf. In the restaurants, we toast it and serve with jam and peanut butter, but at home I enjoy it even more, cold the day after baking, thickly spread with good butter and a sprinkle of sea salt.

Soak the dates and bicarbonate of soda in 115ml boiling water for 30 minutes until soft. Lightly mash the dates and soaking water.

Meanwhile, soak the chia seeds in 2–3 tablespoons water for 15 minutes.

Preheat the oven to 180°C. Grease and line a 21 x 10cm loaf tin with baking paper.

Put all the remaining ingredients in a large bowl and mix together well. Add the chia seeds, then fold in the dates.

Pour into the loaf tin and cook for 1 hour, or until a skewer poked into the centre comes out clean. Leave to cool before slicing. Cut into around 15 slices and store in an airtight container in the fridge for up to 3 days.

Pineapple lamingtons

Makes 20

250g butter, softened
225g self-raising flour
175g golden caster sugar
3 tablespoons desiccated coconut
200g coconut yoghurt
3 large eggs, lightly beaten
200g pineapple (fresh or tinned),
finely chopped

White chocolate icing

450g icing sugar, sifted
100ml milk
20g unsalted butter
175g white chocolate, chopped

Coconut dusting

175g desiccated coconut

We have a bit of a joke in our house that when celebrities are quizzed about their daily diet they often list 'one naughty square of dark chocolate' as their treat. As a self-confessed chocolate addict, I have tried hard to love dark chocolate. I have absolutely no problem stopping at one square — because then I hurry to get the block of white chocolate, and eat my way through it. This baked Australian classic, usually sandwiched with jam and coated in dark chocolate icing before the coconut, pays homage to my secret passion.

You could use the pulp of 3 passionfruit here instead of the pineapple, and coat the squares with warm apricot jam, instead of the icing, to save time.

Preheat the oven to 180°C. Grease and line a deep 20 x 30cm baking tray.

Beat the butter, flour, sugar, coconut, yoghurt and eggs until well combined. Fold in the pineapple, then spoon the mixture into the tin.

Bake for 30 minutes, or until a skewer poked into the centre comes out clean. Leave to cool completely.

Meanwhile, to make the icing, put the icing sugar, milk, butter and chocolate in a large heatproof bowl set over a pan of barely simmering water and stir until melted and smooth. Remove and leave to cool to room temperature.

Cut the cake into 20 equal pieces. Put the desiccated coconut for dusting in a shallow bowl. Dip each cake square into the white chocolate icing and then roll in the coconut to coat. Leave on a wire rack to dry completely before serving.

Spinach, pine nut & feta buns

Makes 18

Dough

85g unsalted butter, diced
675g plain flour, plus extra for dusting
1½ teaspoons salt
375ml milk
2 tablespoons Greek yoghurt
1 egg, lightly beaten
3 teaspoons instant yeast

200g baby spinach, chopped
75g pine nuts, toasted
200g feta cheese, crumbled
Light-flavoured oil, for greasing
1 egg, lightly beaten, to glaze
3 tablespoons grated parmesan

I'm always trying to come up with savoury breakfast foods, rather than sweet muffins, that we can grab on the run. These started life as an answer to that and quickly became a favourite. They're as much filling as dough, which feels good, and are great as part of a weekend brunch spread. In the restaurant we serve them with olive oil and sumac for dipping.

To make the dough, rub the butter into the flour and salt in a large bowl until the mixture resembles breadcrumbs.

Heat the milk in a pan until almost at boiling point, then quickly pour into a separate bowl. Add the yoghurt, egg and yeast and whisk to combine. Pour into the breadcrumb mixture and stir to form a very sticky dough. Cover the bowl and leave to rise for 1 hour.

Knead the dough on a floured surface for a few seconds to knock out any air. Cover and leave in a warm place for a further 15 minutes.

Roll out the dough on a floured surface into a 40 x 30cm rectangle. Scatter with spinach, pine nuts and feta, then roll up tightly like a swiss roll and cut into 18 portions.

Lightly oil a large baking tray. Arrange the buns on the tray with 1cm between them for spreading. Cover with a tea towel and leave to rise for 30 minutes. Preheat the oven to 220°C.

Brush the buns with the egg and sprinkle with parmesan. Bake for 18–20 minutes or until cooked through.

Tip

Freeze any left-over buns and then reheat from frozen. Great in a lunch box, instead of a sandwich.

Yuzu, poppy seed & black sesame loaf with yuzu curd

Makes 10 slices

Loaf

250g butter, softened
250g caster sugar
4 eggs
250g self-raising flour
40g toasted black sesame seeds, lightly crushed
30g poppy seeds
1 tablespoon buttermilk

Yuzu syrup

100ml yuzu juice
50g caster sugar

Yuzu curd

Zest and juice of 1 lemon
Zest and juice of 1 lime
100ml yuzu juice
100g caster sugar
50g butter
2 eggs, plus 1 egg yolk

Yuzu is a classic flavour in Japan. It's a citrus fruit – like a cross between an ugly lemon and a grapefruit – and is reasonably hard to buy outside Japan, although you can easily get the juice, which is all you need here. If you can't find yuzu juice, use grapefruit juice instead. I like to keep my pantry fairly simple and unfussy, so when I find a new flavour, I have to decide after the initial flirtation whether it's going to be a long-term relationship. Yuzu is a keeper. It blends perfectly with the more traditional flavours in this loaf.

Line a 21 x 10cm loaf tin with baking paper. Preheat the oven to 180°C.

To make the loaf, cream the butter and sugar together until white and fluffy. Beat in the eggs one by one – the mixture will split each time but beat it back together again. Gently fold in the flour and sesame and poppy seeds. Stir in the buttermilk to loosen the mixture a little.

Spoon into the tin and bake for 40–45 minutes or until a skewer comes out clean when poked into the centre.

Meanwhile, for the syrup, gently warm the yuzu juice and sugar in a pan, stirring until dissolved. Simmer the yuzu syrup until slightly reduced and thickened.

While the loaf is still warm, pierce the top all over with the skewer. Brush the yuzu syrup over the top to soak in. Leave to cool in the tin.

To make the yuzu curd, whisk together all the ingredients in a pan over low heat, whisking continuously to prevent scrambling. When the mixture has thickened, blend with a stick blender to remove any lumps before serving. Can be stored in an airtight container in the fridge for up to 3 days.

Oat, apricot & macadamia cookies

Makes 12

155g butter, softened
225g caster sugar
2 eggs
225g plain flour
½ teaspoon baking powder
115g ground almonds
½ teaspoon salt
115g rolled oats
70g dried apricots, roughly chopped
115g macadamia nuts, roughly chopped

The Anzac biscuit is an all-time Australian favourite, made with oats and golden syrup. This is a play on that. Macadamias became popular in Australia in the 1980s — until then I only remember seeing them in gift boxes at airports for tourists to take home. For the average city Aussie they were just some nuts we grew locally and hadn't taken much notice of. It seems the macadamia had to make it big overseas before we appreciated it at home — just like so many Australian pop stars.

Beat the butter and sugar together until white and creamy. Add the eggs and beat again.

Stir in the flour, baking powder, ground almonds and salt. Then stir in the oats, apricots and macadamia nuts. Wrap the dough in baking paper and refrigerate for 30 minutes.

Preheat the oven to 180°C. Line 2 large baking trays with baking paper.

Drop heaped tablespoons of dough onto the baking trays, leaving at least 5cm between them to allow for spreading. Bake for 10–12 minutes, until dry-looking and covered with even cracks.

Leave to cool and firm on the trays for 2 minutes. Peel away from the paper and cool completely on a wire rack.

Spiced cauliflower, potato & feta bourekas with date molasses

Makes 12

2 large potatoes (about 500g), peeled and cut into small dice

1 small cauliflower (about 600g), finely diced

4 tablespoons olive oil

2 teaspoons fenugreek seeds

2 teaspoons mustard seeds

2 teaspoons coriander seeds

2 teaspoons fennel seeds

2 teaspoons cumin seeds

2 teaspoons nigella seeds

1 red onion, grated

2.5cm piece fresh ginger, peeled and grated

2 garlic cloves, grated

1 large handful coriander, chopped

150g feta, finely diced

Juice of ½ lemon

12 sheets filo pastry

100g butter, melted

To serve

Seeds from 1 small pomegranate

4 tablespoons date molasses

200g Greek yoghurt

Bourekas are Israeli pastry parcels. Yotam Ottolenghi made Israeli food a global favourite, and Australia has embraced it enthusiastically — the food ethos seems similarly open to all comers and all tastes. This was brought home when an Israeli friend told me: 'Our food is so good because people from all over the world come here to make love in the kitchen.'

Preheat the oven to 180°C. Put the potato and cauliflower in a large bowl and add the oil and spices. Stir to coat.

Spread on a large baking tray and roast for 20 minutes, stirring after 10 minutes. Stir in the grated onion, ginger and garlic and bake for a further 10 minutes, then allow to cool. Stir in the coriander, feta and lemon juice. Divide the filling into 12 portions.

Increase the oven to 200°C. Grease a large baking tray. Unroll the filo sheets and (working with one sheet at a time so they don't dry out) cut in half lengthways. Brush each half with melted butter, then lay one half on top of the other.

Place one portion of filling on the end of the pastry and flatten lightly with your hand. Fold one corner up and over the filling to make a triangle, and fold the other way to reinforce the triangle, and repeat until you have a filled pastry triangle.

Butter the outside of the pastry and lay on the tray. Fill all 12 pastries and then bake for 25 minutes, or until golden.

Meanwhile, put the pomegranate seeds in a small frying pan with half the date molasses and bubble over medium heat until the seeds start to pop. Swirl the remaining date molasses into the yoghurt. Serve both with the pastries.

Tip

You can freeze the unbaked pastries for up to a month. Defrost before baking.

Passionfruit shortbreads

Makes 20

500g butter, softened
240g soft brown sugar
1 teaspoon vanilla extract
440g plain flour
140g cornflour
Pulp of 4 passionfruit
125g ground almonds

Passionfruit icing
Pulp of 2 passionfruit
115g icing sugar, sifted
Edible flower petals

When I got my first home in Australia I was given a passionfruit vine. I planted it in the front yard and within a year it had climbed all over the fence and we were picking the fruit. This extremely crisp butter shortbread might have Scottish origins, but the passionfruit gives it an Aussie flavour.

Beat the butter, sugar and a pinch of salt until pale.

Add the vanilla and beat again. Fold in the flour, cornflour, passionfruit and ground almonds until combined.

Divide the dough into 4 portions. Roll out each portion between sheets of baking paper and refrigerate for 20 minutes. Preheat the oven to 160°C and line a large baking tray with baking paper.

Use a 6cm cutter to cut the dough into rounds. Arrange on the baking tray and bake for 25–30 minutes.

Leave to cool and firm on the trays for 2 minutes. Peel away from the paper and cool completely on a wire rack.

To make the icing, sieve the passionfruit pulp over the icing sugar and stir until smooth. Add some of the seeds too, if you like. Spoon over the shortbread, allow to dry slightly for a couple of minutes and then decorate with edible flowers.

Salted peanut butter & chocolate cookies

Makes 14

200g smooth peanut butter
225g golden caster sugar
2 eggs, lightly beaten
155g plain flour
½ teaspoon baking powder
½ teaspoon salt
100g dark chocolate, roughly chopped
30g salted roasted peanuts, roughly chopped
2 teaspoons sugar

This is the perfect café-style cookie — crunchy and chunky for enjoying with an afternoon cup of tea.

When did we start adding salt to chocolate and caramel? As a chocolate-lover, I realise it is just another ploy to make chocolate even more addictive. Which is possibly not a good thing (although I generally push that thought aside and soldier on).

Beat the peanut butter and caster sugar together with a wooden spoon until well combined. Add the eggs and beat again. Stir in the flour, baking powder and salt. Stir in the chocolate.

Wrap the dough in plastic, roll into a log and refrigerate for 30 minutes. Preheat the oven to 180°C. Line 2 large baking trays with baking paper.

Cut the dough into about 14 slices and arrange on the baking trays, leaving at least 5cm space between them for spreading. Sprinkle with the chopped peanuts and sugar. Bake for 10–12 minutes, until dry-looking and covered with cracks.

Leave to cool and firm on the trays for 2 minutes. Peel away from the paper and cool completely on a wire rack.

Seeded hazelnut rye loaf

Makes 12–15 slices

100g milled linseeds
250g rye flour
125g oatmeal
100g hazelnuts
1 teaspoon sea salt
60g pepitas (pumpkin seeds)
100g runny honey
3 tablespoons light-flavoured oil,
plus extra for greasing

Sometimes I think I'm a frustrated Scandinavian – maybe it's the blond hair or just too much time spent in Ikea. I always feel their style of food works well in Australia, despite being literally on the other side of the world and light whenever we are dark. I love this bread so much I could eat half the loaf in one sitting, which I'm sure negates all the benefits. Rye bread spread with ricotta is my favourite, as shown here, with Scandi-style smoked salmon and dill on top for brunch.

Preheat the oven to 180°C. Line a 21 x 10cm loaf tin with baking paper and grease lightly with oil.

Stir together the linseeds, rye flour, oatmeal, hazelnuts, salt and pepitas in a large bowl.

Combine the honey, oil and 350ml warm water in a jug. Pour into the dry ingredients and stir well to combine. Spoon into the loaf tin.

Bake for 1 hour 20 minutes, or until a skewer poked into the centre comes out clean. Leave to cool in the tin, then turn out to cool completely for a few hours, or until the next day. Slice thinly and toast to serve. Store in an airtight container.

Pistachio & olive oil friands with orange blossom frosting

Makes 10

3 eggs, lightly beaten
200g caster sugar
1 teaspoon vanilla extract
120ml olive oil
100g butter, melted
200g ground pistachios
55g polenta
55g plain flour
1 teaspoon baking powder

Orange blossom frosting

150g cream cheese, softened
½ teaspoon vanilla extract
75g Greek yoghurt
25g icing sugar, sifted
½ teaspoon orange blossom water
55g pistachios, roughly chopped,
to decorate
Freeze-dried raspberry powder,
to decorate

Even though friands are a traditional French cake, they've become an Australian café classic. This recipe uses ground pistachio nuts, rather than the traditional almonds. The pistachio gives the cakes a beautiful pale-green colour.

Preheat the oven to 170°C. Grease ten 150ml silicon moulds or friand tins.

Whisk together the eggs, sugar and vanilla extract. Combine the olive oil and butter and slowly add to the egg mixture, whisking constantly.

Mix the ground pistachios, polenta, flour and baking powder together. Add to the mixture, whisking constantly until just combined. This is a wet batter, so do not be tempted to add more flour.

Pour the batter into the moulds and bake for 15 minutes or until a skewer poked into the centre comes out clean. To help the friands keep their green colour, put a roasting tin of water in the bottom of your oven while you bake them (this will prevent browning).

To make the frosting, beat the cream cheese to soften. Beat in the vanilla and yoghurt until smooth. Beat in the icing sugar and then the orange blossom water.

Spread the frosting onto the friands, then scatter with chopped pistachios and freeze-dried raspberry powder to serve.

Brunch flatbreads

Serves 4

Flatbreads

450g plain flour
2 teaspoons sea salt
1 teaspoon dried yeast
2 tablespoons extra virgin olive oil,
plus a little extra for brushing

Toppings

Caramelised onions, fresh tomato slices,
cherry tomatoes, passata, feta, olives,
pesto, sausage (sliced or pushed out of
its skin), shredded chard leaves, chilli
flakes, dried or fresh herbs

As a student I always looked forward to buying Turkish flatbread pizzas in Sydney's Cleveland Street, usually with spicy sausage on top. If you're having people for brunch, and don't want to be in a production line making toast for a crowd, flatbreads are very easy (quite unlike normal bread dough). Throw whatever you like on these: that could be tomato passata, like a pizza, or caramelised onions, feta, olives, or finely sliced fresh tomatoes with dried oregano and olive oil. You can even top them with a fried egg. Or just a half jar of leftover pesto. Anything that's intensely savoury will work here. You're going to be eating it hot, and it might well involve melted cheese — so it's bound to be good.

To make the flatbreads, sift the flour and salt into a large bowl and make a well in the centre. Stir the yeast and oil into 330ml lukewarm water and pour into the well. Mix to form a soft but firm dough, then tip out onto a lightly floured surface and knead for 5 minutes, or until smooth and elastic.

Put the dough in a lightly oiled bowl, cover and leave to rise in a warm place for 45 minutes.

Preheat your oven to 220°C and knock back the dough by punching it with your fist. Divide it into 4 equal balls and roll each one into a long oval about 3–4mm thick. Place on an oiled baking tray.

Brush the flatbreads with a little more oil and arrange your toppings on them. We used sliced red onion, grated haloumi, sausage pushed out of the skin, and halved cherry tomatoes.

Bake the flatbreads in the hot oven for 20 minutes. Once baked, top with fresh herbs, or more grated cheese, chilli flakes or just a twist of black pepper and serve immediately.

Bowls

Fragrant chicken broth with brown rice, mushrooms, lime & coriander

Serves 4

Poached chicken

1 litre chicken stock

3 spring onions, lightly crushed

60g fresh ginger, peeled and thinly sliced

1 lemongrass stalk, white part only, bruised

1 bunch coriander roots

2 large chicken breasts (250g each)

Herb paste

1 large handful parsley

½ handful chervil

½ handful coriander

2 tablespoons olive oil

To serve

1.5 litres good-quality chicken broth

1 small bunch cavolo nero or kale, finely shredded

Cooked brown rice (about 2 cupfuls)

280g king oyster mushrooms, sliced

1 handful beansprouts

½ white onion, finely sliced, soaked in water

1 spring onion, finely sliced

1 large handful coriander

2 tablespoons chopped chives

2 limes, cut into wedges

The first time I tasted this variation of the rice bowl, piled high with herbs and sitting in broth, was 15 years ago at the wonderful restaurant Axe in Venice, LA. It was the era of 'my body is a temple' and Axe was temple food at its best – simple, pure and monastic. This is my version.

To poach the chicken, put the stock, spring onions, ginger, lemongrass, coriander roots and chicken in a large pan over medium–high heat and bring to a high simmer. Reduce the heat and simmer gently for 15 minutes, or until the chicken is cooked through. Leave to cool in the liquid, then shred the chicken into bite-sized pieces and discard the liquid.

Meanwhile, make the herb paste. Mix the herbs in a blender with the oil and 2 tablespoons water until smooth. Season with sea salt and freshly ground black pepper to taste. You can make this in advance – it keeps for 2 days in the fridge.

Put the broth in a pan over medium heat. Add the cavolo nero and shredded chicken and heat through. Spoon into bowls and add rice to each bowl. Top up with more broth.

Add the mushrooms, beansprouts, white onion, spring onion and coriander. Finish each bowl with a spoonful of herb paste, chopped chives and lime wedges.

Coconut fish curry

Serves 4

Fish curry

1 tablespoon chilli flakes

1 tablespoon Korean chilli flakes

2 red chillies

3 garlic cloves

2 French shallots, peeled

70g fresh ginger, peeled and roughly chopped

2 lemongrass stalks, white part only, bruised and roughly chopped

1 tablespoon curry powder

1 tablespoon ground cumin

1 tablespoon ground coriander

1 heaped teaspoon shrimp paste

Light-flavoured oil

60g palm sugar, crumbled or grated

3 tablespoons tamarind purée

400ml coconut milk

10 makrut lime leaves

1kg barramundi fillet, cut into bite-sized pieces

To serve

1 cucumber, sliced into thin ribbons

50g fresh ginger, peeled and finely chopped

1 small handful holy basil

1 small handful coriander

1 bunch gai larn (Chinese broccoli), stalks removed, blanched

1 tablespoon sambal ranggup ikan bilis

1 lemon, cut into wedges

Steamed brown rice

When we opened Granger & Co in Notting Hill in November 2011, I was very conscious of the menu needing to bring the sunshine of Australia, while being appropriate for the dark and rather chilly London autumn. Grilled fish with a tangy salad was perfect for Sydney, but London needed warming up. This curry is what we came up with, and it's been on the menu ever since. This is a mix-up of different ideas and non-traditional cuisines — which is how this Aussie was feeling after being in London for a couple of years.

To make the curry, blend the aromatics, spices and shrimp paste with a little oil to make a very smooth curry paste.

Heat a little more oil in a large heavy-based pan and cook the paste over low heat for 6–8 minutes until it starts to deepen in colour. Add the palm sugar and cook until fully dissolved. Add the tamarind and cook for 3–5 minutes.

Add the coconut milk and 600ml water with the lime leaves and simmer for 20–30 minutes until the sauce has deepened in flavour and colour.

Add the fish to the sauce and heat through for 5–6 minutes until the fish is cooked.

To serve, toss together the cucumber, ginger, basil and coriander to make a salad. Arrange the gai larn in 4 bowls, spoon in the curry and garnish with the cucumber salad.

Serve with ikan bilis, lemon wedges and brown rice.

Green tea & aonori-seared tuna with soba noodles & ponzu

Serves 4

360g centre-cut sashimi-grade tuna fillet

4 tablespoons light-flavoured oil, plus extra for brushing

½ teaspoon green tea powder

2g dried aonori flakes

8 shiso leaves

Ponzu dressing

1 tablespoon sesame oil

2 tablespoons ponzu sauce (citrus soy)

1½ tablespoons mirin

1 tablespoon lemon juice

To serve

1 zucchini (courgette), sliced into noodles or ribbons

200g soba noodles, cooked according to the packet instructions

1 bunch coriander leaves

1 small punnet baby shiso cress

This is inspired by the summer noodle dish, hiyashi chuka, that I ate in ramen bars as a student. I put my version on our first menus, using soba noodles instead of ramen, and seared pink tuna instead of shredded processed pink ham. I am yet to be convinced that spiralised zucchini (courgette) is a complete replacement for pasta, but here its raw nuttiness does give a delicious contrast.

Brush the piece of tuna with a little oil. Mix the green tea powder and aonori together with a pinch of sea salt and rub all over the tuna.

Heat 2 tablespoons of the oil in a large frying pan until smoking hot. Sear the tuna on all sides, then lift onto a plate.

While the pan is still hot, add the remaining 2 tablespoons oil, heat until very hot and quickly fry the shiso leaves, turning once, until translucent. Lift out onto kitchen paper and season with sea salt.

Using a very sharp knife and working with the grain, slice the tuna into 12 pieces.

To make the ponzu dressing, combine all the ingredients.

To serve, mix the zucchini ribbons and soba noodles with a little ponzu dressing and half the herbs.

Serve the tuna, zucchini ribbons and noodles drizzled with more dressing. Garnish with the remaining herbs and the fried shiso leaves.

Braised lamb ragu with tagliatelle & pecorino

Serves 6

Lamb ragu

Olive oil
1 small lamb shoulder, bone in
(about 1400g)
2 carrots, chopped into large pieces
1 onion, quartered
5 garlic cloves, peeled and roughly
chopped
¼ bunch oregano
10 prunes, pitted
2 tablespoons ground sumac
2 tablespoons fennel seeds
1 litre vegetable stock
250ml white wine

To serve

500g tagliatelle
8 radicchio leaves, finely sliced
150g pecorino, grated
Zest of 2 lemons
1 small bunch parsley, finely chopped

Growing up in the seventies, roast lamb was as much a part of our Australian psyche as milk bars, Vegemite and beetroot on our burgers. In the eighties, Australian lamb was even advertised by a wholesome Aussie girl – Naomi Watts, no less – turning down dinner with Tom Cruise because 'Mum's doing a lamb roast'. As much as I love traditional lamb, the Greeks brought us their meltingly slow-cooked lamb cuts, elevating the meat to new heights. Here I toss it with pasta, but feel free to serve it with carbs of your choice to soak up the juices.

Preheat the oven to 170°C. Place a deep flameproof oven dish on the stovetop over medium–high heat and drizzle generously with olive oil. Season the lamb shoulder with sea salt and freshly ground black pepper and sear on both sides in the dish.

Add all the remaining ragu ingredients, seal the dish with two layers of foil and put in the oven for 5 hours until the lamb is tender and falling off the bone. Cool slightly.

Gently pull apart the lamb, removing and discarding any skin and bones and gently breaking up the carrots and onion. Put the dish on the stovetop over medium heat and simmer until the liquid has reduced by half. Season again, if necessary.

Meanwhile, cook the tagliatelle according to the packet instructions until al dente. Drain and add to the ragu, stirring gently to coat.

Spoon into bowls and serve with radicchio. Sprinkle with pecorino, lemon zest and chopped parsley to serve.

Kale, lemon & pistachio pistou
with spelt spaghetti & garlic pangrattato

Serves 4

Kale, lemon & pistachio pistou

80g kale, stalks removed, blanched

40g spinach, stalks removed, blanched

25g basil, blanched

25g pistachio nuts, toasted

25g grated parmesan

50ml olive oil

1 garlic clove, roughly chopped

½ teaspoon red chilli flakes

Zest and juice of ½ lemon

250g spelt spaghetti

80g kale, stalks removed, roughly chopped

200g broccolini

2 teaspoons olive oil

Squeeze of lemon juice

4 tablespoons grated parmesan

Garlic pangrattato

1 tablespoon olive oil

4 tablespoons sourdough breadcrumbs

2 garlic cloves, finely chopped

How come kids 'don't like green food' but they all seem to love pesto? How food trends change. I remember wanting to make pesto during a home economics lesson at school and I was practically laughed out of the building — in those days we couldn't even buy fresh basil. Try this kale variation as a way to get even more great greens onto everyone's plate. If you have leftover pistou, keep it in an airtight container in the fridge for up to 3 days and add to soups and poached eggs, or spread it over toasted crostini.

To make the pistou, pulse all the ingredients together in a processor with a pinch of salt until a coarse paste forms. Check the seasoning.

Cook the spaghetti according to the packet instructions until al dente. While the pasta cooks, quickly blanch the kale and broccolini in the pan, then drain well.

Meanwhile, to make the garlic pangrattato, heat the olive oil in a pan and toss the breadcrumbs and garlic together over medium heat until crispy.

Drain the pasta, keeping a small cup of the cooking water. Toss the pasta with the olive oil, lemon juice, half the pistou and the cooking water. Add the blanched kale and broccolini and toss to combine. Add more pistou, if needed, to thoroughly coat.

Arrange in bowls and sprinkle with the parmesan and garlic pangrattato.

Green herb risotto with raw summer salad

Serves 4

Raw summer salad

5 asparagus spears, sliced into ribbons

1 zucchini (courgette), sliced into ribbons

6 Brussels sprouts or 2 kale leaves, finely shredded

12 nasturtium leaves

1 tablespoon lemon juice

2 tablespoons extra virgin olive oil

Risotto

50g butter

2 French shallots, finely chopped

3 garlic cloves, finely chopped

1½ tablespoons thyme

400g risotto rice

200ml white wine

1.2 litres warm vegetable stock

Zest and juice of ½ lemon

3 tablespoons grated parmesan

Green herb purée

50g parsley

50g baby spinach

50g rocket

50ml olive oil

I've always loved the idea of nasturtium leaves in a salad. They grow everywhere, and so easily. In the early days of bills our chef used to pick them on the way to work, and now I always grow them in the garden.

The risotto uses a simple but clever method — the green herb mixture is blended and then stirred into the cooked risotto — that way the colours and flavours stay completely fresh and the greens aren't cooked at all. It's almost like saying risotto is good for you. In fact, because the butter and cheese help you absorb the vitamins from the greens, this is practically spa food!

To make the raw summer salad, toss together the asparagus, zucchini, sprouts or kale and nasturtium leaves. Whisk together the lemon juice and oil with sea salt and freshly ground black pepper to make a citrus dressing. Toss the salad with the dressing and set aside until ready to serve.

To make the risotto, heat half the butter in a pan over low–medium heat. Gently cook the shallots, garlic and thyme in the butter until the shallots are soft and translucent. Add the rice and cook, stirring well, for a minute or so, until all the rice is coated in hot butter. Add the white wine and stir until it has all been absorbed. Slowly stir in the warm stock, a ladleful at a time, stirring continuously until it has been absorbed before adding the next ladle — this will take around 20–25 minutes.

To make the green herb purée, mix all the ingredients in a blender until thick and smooth. Season to taste.

Stir the green herb purée into the risotto. Finish with the remaining butter, a squeeze of lemon juice and the parmesan. Serve with the salad, sprinkled with lemon zest.

Crab & chilli linguine

Serves 4

500g linguine
125ml olive oil
4 tablespoons butter
2 French shallots, finely chopped
4 garlic cloves, finely chopped
2 red chillies, finely chopped
200g white crab meat
200g brown crab meat
Zest and juice of 1 lemon
1 large handful parsley, finely chopped
2 teaspoons chilli flakes

This is archetypal Sydney lunch food — the bowl you order with a glass of chilled white wine when you're sitting poolside or at a beach café under a bright blue Australian sky. We've had prawn and chilli linguine on the bills lunch menu since the early days, although we swap it out sometimes for crab and chilli. This is a great blend of Australia's Italian food heritage with sweet crab and a hint of Asian chilli to add spice. Might it be the world's most perfect flavour combination?

Cook the linguine according to the packet instructions until al dente. Drain, reserving half a cupful of the cooking water.

Meanwhile, heat the oil and butter in a large frying pan and gently cook the shallots, garlic and chillies until slightly softened and fragrant. Add the linguine and pasta water and toss gently to completely coat.

Fold in the light and dark crab meat. Stir in the lemon juice and half the parsley and season to taste.

Serve in bowls, sprinkled with the remaining parsley, lemon zest, chilli flakes and freshly ground black pepper.

Chickpea, kale & paneer curry

Serves 4

2 tablespoons light-flavoured oil

200g paneer cheese, cut into cubes

1 onion, chopped

3 garlic cloves, crushed

3cm piece fresh ginger, peeled and grated

1 teaspoon hot curry powder

1 teaspoon ground cumin

1 teaspoon ground turmeric

½ teaspoon dried chilli flakes

2 x 400g tins chickpeas, rinsed

300g curly kale, stalks removed, roughly shredded

400ml vegetable stock

Juice of ½ lemon, plus extra wedges to serve

Steamed white rice, to serve

I always get excited at the idea of Indian takeaway on a Friday night, but afterwards I often feel very full, very sleepy and wake up on the sofa three hours later. So, this is my Australian update: a fresh, light curry you can make at home very easily with tinned chickpeas — it's not too heavy and not too rich, either. I think it's great that we're all eating less meat — this is another excellent dinner for a meat-free day.

Heat a drizzle of oil in a large non-stick frying pan over medium heat. Fry the paneer until warmed through and browned on all sides, remove from the pan and set aside.

Add the remaining oil to the pan and fry the onion for 5 minutes, or until soft. Add the garlic, ginger and spices and fry for 2 minutes, or until fragrant.

Add the chickpeas, kale and stock, stir to coat in the spices and then bubble until the kale is tender and the stock has been absorbed.

Add the lemon juice, fold in the paneer and serve with steamed white rice and lemon wedges.

Cod, turmeric & dill noodles with green chilli relish

Serves 4

3 garlic cloves, crushed

2cm piece fresh ginger, peeled and grated

2 teaspoons ground turmeric

1 tablespoon fish sauce

1 teaspoon caster sugar

600g blue-eyed cod or other firm white fish, cut into chunks, skin removed

½ teaspoon ground white pepper

2 tablespoons light-flavoured oil

1 large bunch dill, roughly chopped

3 spring onions, finely sliced

Juice of ½ lemon

250g rice vermicelli, cooked according to packet instructions

3 tablespoons roasted peanuts, crushed

Green chilli relish

2 tablespoons palm sugar, crumbled or grated

1 green chilli, deseeded and finely chopped

1 garlic clove, finely chopped

Zest and juice of 1 lime

1½ tablespoons fish sauce

1 tablespoon rice wine vinegar

This is my variation on Hanoi fish, which is one of the most fragrant dishes you'll ever come across. This is punchy with big flavours but light to eat — it looks fancy in the bowl but is simple enough to make for a midweek meal with a plate of steamed greens with olive oil, soy and a squeeze of lemon. Use blue-eyed cod or any firm white fish here.

Mix together the garlic, ginger, turmeric, fish sauce and sugar. Stir in the fish, cover and leave to marinate in the fridge for 15 minutes.

Meanwhile, to make the green chilli relish, whisk together all the ingredients until the palm sugar has dissolved.

Season the fish with white pepper. Heat the oil in a large heavy-based frying pan over medium–high heat, add the fish and cook for 2 minutes on each side, turning once. Add 2 tablespoons water and bring to a simmer.

Gently fold in the dill and spring onions. Once they've wilted, remove the pan from the heat and add the lemon juice. Check the seasoning, adding salt if needed.

Serve the fish with the noodles, peanuts and green chilli relish in separate bowls for everyone to help themselves.

Braised tofu & mushrooms with black beans & chilli tomato sauce

Serves 4

Szechuan salt

1 teaspoon fennel seeds
1 teaspoon Szechuan peppercorns
1 teaspoon sea salt

Chilli tomato sauce

2 tablespoons light-flavoured oil
50g fresh ginger, peeled and finely chopped
50g finely chopped garlic
700g cherry tomatoes, halved
100g chilli bean paste
100g fermented Korean bean paste (doenjang)

2 tablespoons light-flavoured oil
250g chopped mixed mushrooms
400g firm tofu, cut into 2cm dice
100g edamame beans
60g soaked fermented black beans
1 small bunch coriander, chopped
1 spring onion, finely chopped
1 tablespoon crispy shallots
Steamed rice, to serve

This is very loosely inspired by the mapo tofu that we used to eat after work, late at night, at Golden Century in Sydney's Chinatown. It's usually made with minced pork as well as the tofu, but I would order the vegetarian version, which is sticky and soothing after a long day. This is another great dish for vegans.

To make the Szechuan salt. toast the fennel seeds and peppercorns in a dry pan for 5 minutes over low heat. Put in a spice grinder with the salt and grind to a powder (you can keep this in an airtight container for up to 4 weeks).

To make the chilli tomato sauce, heat the oil in a pan and add the ginger. Cook until slightly coloured, then add the garlic. Add the tomatoes, let them blister and release their juice, then add bean pastes. Stir in 100ml hot water, a little at a time. Simmer for 5–10 minutes, until the sauce has a rich consistency.

Meanwhile, heat the oil in a pan and add the mushrooms and tofu. Cook until the tofu is just crisp, then add the edamame and black beans and heat through gently. Add to the chilli tomato sauce and stir through.

Spoon into bowls and garnish with coriander, spring onion, crispy shallots and a sprinkle of Szechuan salt. Serve with steamed rice.

Duck ragu with umeboshi mushrooms & pappardelle

Serves 4

Duck ragu

Olive oil, for frying
3 large duck Marylands (leg and thigh), around 350g each
2 French shallots, sliced
5 garlic cloves, sliced
250ml white wine
500ml chicken stock
1 fennel bulb, sliced
3 bay leaves
5 thyme sprigs
2 carrots, cut in half

Umeboshi mushrooms

1 tablespoon truffle oil
2 tablespoons umeboshi plums, crushed
1 tablespoon red wine vinegar
1½ tablespoons white rice vinegar
1 teaspoon fish sauce
1 tablespoon tamari
4 tablespoons light-flavoured oil
250g mixed Asian mushrooms
100g rocket

To serve

375g pappardelle
1 tablespoon softened butter
Truffle oil

It sometimes feels as if the Japanese can do everything better than the rest of us, and they have no worries about cultural appropriation — they make hamburgers tastier than the Americans, German cakes richer than the originals, and pasta better than the Italians. Japanese wafu (Western fusion) pasta is umami flavoured and delicious and the star of our menus in Japan. Umeboshi is a Japanese salt-preserved plum bought in jars.

To make the duck ragu, heat a little olive oil in a flameproof oven dish over medium–high heat and brown the duck legs all over. Remove to a plate to cool. Add the shallots and garlic to the dish and stir for 1 minute. Add the wine and stock and bring to a simmer. Preheat the oven to 180°C.

Return the duck legs to the oven dish and add the fennel, bay leaves, thyme and carrots. Cover with a lid or foil and put in the oven for 2½ hours.

Remove the carrot and bay leaves from the dish and discard. Remove the duck legs and allow to cool, then remove the skin and bones and shred the duck. Return the duck meat to the sauce in the dish and check for seasoning.

Meanwhile, to make the umeboshi mushrooms, mix the truffle oil and crushed umeboshi in a bowl. Slowly whisk in the vinegars, fish sauce, tamari and half the oil to make a dressing.

Heat the remaining oil in a pan over medium heat and sauté the mushrooms for 2 minutes. Turn off the heat and add the dressing and rocket. Toss well.

Meanwhile, cook the pappardelle according to the packet instructions until al dente. Drain and toss with the butter.

Serve the pasta topped with the duck ragu and umeboshi mushrooms. Drizzle with truffle oil to serve.

Tuna & avocado poke bowl
with samphire & sesame

Serves 4

2 teaspoons sesame oil

2 tablespoons soy sauce

2 tablespoons mirin

4cm piece fresh ginger, peeled and finely chopped

2 spring onions, very finely chopped

320g sashimi-grade tuna, cut into 2cm dice

1 teaspoon each white and black sesame seeds, toasted

40g samphire or 2 asparagus spears, finely sliced

160g cherry tomatoes, halved

300g cooked short-grain brown rice

2 avocados, chopped

4 tablespoons pickled ginger or cucumber

1 handful coriander leaves

4 teaspoons furikake (Japanese nori sesame topping)

1 lime, cut into wedges

The poke bowl of fresh ingredients and sliced raw fish came from my first trip to Hawaii. I loved the idea and put it on the menu straightaway. Sales were slow at first: a 'poke' is an Australian euphemism for something else, so it caused confusion on the Sydney menu before becoming a huge trend. Hawaiian poke bowls work perfectly with our Australian food ethos of arranging the best flavours together and not mucking around with them too much.

Whisk together the sesame oil, soy sauce, mirin, ginger and spring onions to make a dressing.

Place the tuna in a bowl with the sesame seeds, samphire or asparagus, cherry tomatoes and most of the dressing and toss together gently.

Spoon the rice into 4 bowls and pour on the remaining dressing. Add the tuna mixture. Finish each bowl with half an avocado, some pickled ginger or cucumber, coriander and a sprinkling of furikake. Serve with lime wedges.

Yellow split pea & turmeric dhal with date & tamarind chutney

Serves 4–6

1 onion, roughly chopped
8cm piece fresh ginger, peeled and roughly chopped
3 garlic cloves, roughly chopped
5cm piece fresh turmeric
4 tablespoons light-flavoured oil
3 teaspoons fenugreek seeds
3 teaspoons yellow mustard seeds
3 teaspoons ground coriander
3 teaspoons ground cumin
1½ teaspoons chilli powder
250g yellow split peas
600ml coconut milk
6 makrut lime leaves

Date & tamarind chutney

3 tablespoons olive oil
3 garlic cloves, roughly chopped
2.5cm piece fresh ginger, peeled and roughly chopped
1 French shallot, roughly chopped
1 tablespoon each fennel seeds, mustard seeds, cumin seeds
1 tablespoon cardamom pods, crushed
2 teaspoons cayenne pepper
2 teaspoons Chinese five-spice
3 tablespoons miso paste
100g soft brown sugar
75ml black rice vinegar
125g tamarind paste
100g pitted dates, roughly chopped
2 plums, roughly chopped
1 apple, roughly chopped

To serve

1 large handful mint, chopped
1 large handful coriander, chopped
1 green chilli, sliced
Coconut yoghurt
Pickles, optional

I can eat dhal at any time of the day. In my art school days, my friends and I loved going to the Hare Krishna restaurant, where we could get a great vegetarian meal and watch a film, all for $3. The unspoken price, of course, was some politely gentle attempts at religious conversion. I would always feel a bit guilty as we sat on the floor eating our dhal, but now this is my idea of true comfort food. The chutney lifts this above the everyday, but could easily be bought if you are short of time.

Put the onion, ginger, garlic and turmeric in a food processor and mix to a rough paste.

Heat the oil in a large heavy-based pan over medium heat. When the oil is hot, add the paste, fenugreek seeds and mustard seeds. Cook for 5 minutes, stirring frequently, until the paste is fragrant. Add the ground coriander, cumin and chilli powder and cook for a further minute.

Pour the split peas and coconut milk into the pan along with 500ml cold water. Add the makrut lime leaves. Bring to the boil, simmer strongly for 10 minutes, stirring frequently, then reduce the heat and simmer gently for 45 minutes, stirring to prevent sticking. If it looks dry, add more water.

Meanwhile, to make the chutney, heat the olive oil in a heavy-based pan over medium heat. Add the garlic, ginger, shallot, fennel seeds, mustard seeds and cumin seeds. Cook, stirring occasionally for 10 minutes until the shallot is translucent. Add the cardamom, cayenne and five-spice and cook for a further minute.

Add the remaining ingredients with 500ml water. Bring to the boil, then reduce the heat to simmer for 10–12 minutes or until the fruit is very soft and the chutney is rich dark brown. Leave to cool for 5 minutes. Blend until completely smooth. This makes around 16 serves of chutney that will keep in an airtight container in the fridge for up to a month – delicious with cold meats, cheeses, pies and all curries.

Serve the dhal and chutney with mint, coriander, chilli, a dollop of coconut yoghurt and perhaps some pickles.

Salads

Poached salmon with freekeh, zoodles & charred tomato dressing

Serves 4

Charred tomato dressing
Zest and juice of ½ lemon
3 tablespoons olive oil
200g cherry tomatoes, halved

200g cracked freekeh
750ml hot vegetable stock
4 x 140g salmon pieces
200g Greek yoghurt
Zest and juice of ½ lemon
1 tablespoon softened butter
2 large zucchini (courgettes),
spiralised or shaved into ribbons
1 small bunch basil
2 teaspoons ground sumac
Extra virgin olive oil, to drizzle

I love salmon and it almost always makes it into at least one weeknight dinner in our home. I have two favourite ways to cook it: crispy skinned in the oven, or, if I'm feeling virtuous, poached, with a yoghurt dressing. Salmon is very forgiving of the nervous cook — it can happily survive a bit of under- or over-cooking, unlike white fish. You can serve this at room temperature. The sumac adds an extra layer of flavour.

To make the charred tomato dressing, combine the lemon zest, juice and 2 tablespoons of olive oil in a bowl.

Heat the remaining oil in a pan until smoking hot. Add the tomatoes and leave to blister and darken for 3–4 minutes, moving only slightly so that they char evenly, and adding more oil if needed. Once charred, add the tomatoes to the oil and lemon, season to taste and leave for at least 1 hour for the flavours to develop.

Put the freekeh and stock in a saucepan and bring to the boil. Reduce the heat and simmer for 15 minutes, stirring occasionally, until the freekeh has softened and the stock has been absorbed.

Meanwhile, poach the salmon. Fill a deep frying pan with salted water and bring to a simmer. Add the salmon to the water and simmer for 5–6 minutes until the salmon is pink and firm-ish. Remove from the water and leave to rest.

Mix together the yoghurt, lemon zest, juice and plenty of freshly ground black pepper.

Heat the butter in a frying pan until just starting to sizzle and add the zucchini noodles. Toss gently in the butter for a minute or two, until just starting to soften. Remove from the heat and pour in the charred tomato dressing. Stir gently and check the seasoning.

Serve the freekeh and zucchini noodles with the flaked salmon and a spoonful of lemon yoghurt. Sprinkle with basil leaves, sumac and a little extra virgin olive oil to serve.

Summer chopped salad with citrus sesame dressing

Serves 4

2 corn cobs
1 tablespoon olive oil
2 small zucchini (courgettes), chopped
¼ small white cabbage, finely sliced
2 small Lebanese cucumbers, chopped
2 small beetroot, cooked and cut into wedges
1 small iceberg lettuce, roughly chopped
4 tablespoons apple cider vinegar
120g edamame beans, blanched
1 small handful dill
1 small handful parsley
2 spring onions, finely chopped
4 tablespoons furikake (Japanese nori sesame topping)

Citrus sesame dressing

1 garlic clove, finely chopped
1½ tablespoons tahini
1 tablespoon tamari
3 tablespoons rice wine vinegar
1 tablespoon ponzu sauce (citrus soy)
2 tablespoons light-flavoured oil
1 teaspoon sesame oil
1 tablespoon wasabi paste
1 red Asian shallot, finely diced

Deep-fried chickpeas

500ml light-flavoured oil, for deep-frying
400g tin chickpeas, drained
1 tablespoon furikake (Japanese nori sesame topping)

My favourite go-to lunch is always a chopped salad. I love that you can eat it just with a fork. Serve this as it is or with haloumi, chicken, tofu or salmon. But, like any salad, the best part about this dish is the dressing. This is magic dressing, with a creaminess that isn't cream.

Cut the corn cobs in half and simmer in a large pan of water for 8 minutes, then drain and cool. Cut off the kernels.

Heat a little olive oil in a hot pan, add the corn kernels and zucchini and cook until the zucchini is just starting to soften and colour.

Meanwhile, make the citrus sesame dressing. Whisk the garlic, tahini, tamari, vinegar and ponzu in a bowl. Slowly add the oils, whisking continuously until emulsified. Whisk in the wasabi and then stir in the shallot.

To deep-fry the chickpeas, heat the oil in a large heavy-based pan until a breadcrumb dropped in sizzles and dances on the top of the oil. Carefully add the chickpeas and fry for 2 minutes, or until they start to blister. Drain in a bowl lined with kitchen paper. Season with the furikake while still hot and then leave to cool down completely. (You can store them in an airtight container for up to a day – they make an excellent snack.)

Arrange the white cabbage, cucumber, beetroot and lettuce in a bowl, add the apple cider vinegar and toss well. Arrange the corn, zucchini and edamame on top.

Drizzle the sesame dressing over the salad and finish with the chickpeas, dill, parsley, spring onions and furikake.

Winter chopped salad with peanut & lime dressing

Serves 4

Crispy peanuts

100g blanched peanuts
1 teaspoon olive oil
1 teaspoon soft brown sugar
1 teaspoon coarse sea salt
1 lemongrass stalk, white part only, bruised and finely chopped
2 makrut lime leaves, stalks removed, finely sliced
1 teaspoon chilli flakes

Peanut & lime dressing

4 tablespoons smooth peanut butter
4 tablespoons coconut milk
Juice of 1 lime
1½ tablespoons tamari soy sauce
2 teaspoons maple syrup

1 kohlrabi, cut into matchsticks
1 iceberg lettuce, torn into quarters
250g cherry tomatoes, halved
2 Lebanese cucumbers, chopped
100g sprouting seeds
150g edamame beans, blanched
1 large yellow beetroot, steamed, peeled and diced
¼ red cabbage, finely sliced
2 tablespoons lemon juice
3 tablespoons extra virgin olive oil
1 bunch each dill, coriander and mint

Don't forget to be adventurous with your salad ingredients and use whatever's in season. It really is decades since we saw salad as 'only' a summer dish. Keep the textures crisp and the dressing warming and serve this with roast chicken or warm haloumi on a winter's day... even a London winter's day.

To make the crispy peanuts, preheat the oven to 180°C. Mix the nuts with the oil, sugar and salt in a roasting tin and roast for 12 minutes, or until starting to colour. Toss with the chopped lemongrass and sliced lime leaves, return to the oven and cook for a further 4 minutes or until golden brown. Toss through the chilli flakes. Leave to cool and then gently crush the peanuts. These will keep for 5 days in an airtight container.

To make the peanut dressing, blend all the ingredients together with 2 tablespoons water until smooth.

Arrange the kohlrabi and torn iceberg in 4 bowls, then add the tomatoes, cucumber, sprouting seeds, edamame beans, beetroot and red cabbage.

Whisk together the lemon juice and extra virgin olive oil. Drizzle over the salad and season to taste.

Spoon a little peanut dressing over the top and sprinkle with the crispy nuts. Garnish with herbs and serve the rest of the peanut dressing on the side.

Warm lentil salad with burrata & basil oil

Serves 4

300g puy (blue–green) lentils
100ml olive oil
1 onion, finely chopped
3 garlic cloves, finely chopped
1 celery stalk, finely chopped
1 large tomato, finely diced
1 bouquet garni (2 thyme sprigs,
5 parsley stalks, 2 bay leaves
tied together)
750ml hot vegetable stock
200g baby spinach
50g sourdough bread, diced and
shallow-fried in oil until crisp
300g burrata
Baby beetroot shoots or shiso cress
1 large handful basil

We've always had a lentil salad on the lunch menu in Sydney — even before pulses claimed their rightful place, high in the superfood pecking order. But it was a cold dark London autumn when we opened in Notting Hill; we were far from that Aussie sunshine and we all needed a bit of comfort food. Braising the lentils and serving them warm, with a spoonful of creamy melting burrata, rather than the sharp sea-salty feta we use in Sydney, worked a treat.

Rinse the lentils under running water. Heat 2 tablespoons olive oil in a pan over medium heat, add the onion, garlic and celery and cook gently until translucent.

Add the tomato and cook for a further 3 minutes. Add the lentils and bouquet garni, stir well and then add the stock and reduce the heat. Simmer, stirring occasionally, for 20 minutes or until the lentils are cooked and the stock has been absorbed.

Stir the spinach into the lentils until just wilted and check the seasoning. Transfer to a bowl, scatter with the sourdough croutons and torn burrata and garnish with beetroot shoots.

Mix the basil with the remaining olive oil in a blender, season to taste and drizzle over the salad.

Warm spelt salad with roasted spiced oranges

Serves 4

2 small oranges, unpeeled, finely sliced
1 teaspoon fennel seeds
1 teaspoon cumin seeds
1 teaspoon chilli flakes
2 teaspoons runny honey
4 tablespoons olive oil
200g spelt
1 garlic clove, crushed
Juice of ½ lemon
1 large carrot, grated
1 handful dill, chopped
1 handful mint leaves, chopped

One of the unexpected side-effects of this salad is that roasting the oranges will leave your kitchen smelling spectacular! This is a great festive Christmas dish to serve with roast meats, fish or haloumi. Use thin-skinned oranges as you'll be roasting and eating the whole fruit.

Preheat the oven to 220°C. Line a large oven tray with baking paper and arrange the orange slices in one layer.

Mix the fennel, cumin, chilli and honey with half the oil and season with salt. Spoon over the orange slices, spreading evenly with the back of the spoon. Roast for 15–20 minutes until the oranges are caramelised and slightly charred.

Meanwhile, cook the spelt in boiling salted water for 20 minutes, or until just cooked. Drain and return to the pan. Add the garlic and remaining 2 tablespoons olive oil. Add the lemon juice and toss together well.

Set aside for 10 minutes to cool slightly and then stir in the orange slices, carrot, dill and mint. Season to taste with sea salt and freshly ground black pepper.

Poached chicken salad with nashi pear, watercress & avocado

Serves 4

2 large chicken breasts
800ml coconut milk
3 tablespoons fish sauce
Juice of 2 limes
5 makrut lime leaves
1 bunch watercress
2 nashi pears, julienned
1 teaspoon chilli flakes
2 avocados, halved
2 tablespoons lemon juice
2 tablespoons extra virgin olive oil
2 limes, cut into wedges

This is a lovely fresh salad of simple ingredients with great complimentary flavours. Poaching the chicken in coconut milk is a clever method to prevent it drying out. You can keep the poaching liquid (which can be frozen) and just add paste to make a quick curry.

Put the chicken breasts, coconut milk, fish sauce, lime juice and lime leaves in a small pan, just large enough to fit. Bring to a gentle simmer and poach for 15 minutes, or until the chicken is cooked through. Remove from the heat and leave to cool in the poaching liquid. Finely shred the chicken (save the poaching liquid if you want to use it again).

Toss together the watercress, nashi pear and chilli flakes in a large bowl. Add the chicken and avocado and season well.

Whisk together the lemon juice and extra virgin olive oil to make a dressing and drizzle over the salad. Serve with lime wedges.

Prawn & green mango salad with green nuoc cham

Serves 4

Green nuoc cham

1 bunch coriander stalks

2 green chillies

1 garlic clove

1 tablespoon lime juice

2 tablespoons fish sauce

1 tablespoon palm sugar, crumbled or grated

600g cooked prawns, peeled and deveined

2 green mangoes, julienned

½ kohlrabi, julienned

4 spring onions, finely sliced

1 large bunch each coriander and holy basil

4 tablespoons crispy shallots

1 lime, cut into wedges

A tray of mangoes and a box of cherries — that's an Australian Christmas, right there. Australian mangoes are the best in the world. There is palpable excitement in December when the first trays of fruit start to appear in greengrocers and for sale from the backs of utes on country roads. There are bound to be a few unripe ones in the box you can use for this — you want the tangy sourness, rather than the ripe juicy sweetness. You can also buy raw prawns here and barbecue them first.

To make the nuoc cham, blend all the ingredients together with 2 tablespoons water until smooth.

Gently toss the prawns with the mango, kohlrabi and spring onion in a large bowl. Add the green nuoc cham, coriander and holy basil and garnish with the crispy shallots. Serve with lime wedges.

Butter lettuce, shiso & avocado salad with yuzukosho dressing

Serves 4

Yuzukosho dressing

3 tablespoons olive oil
2 tablespoons rice wine vinegar
2 tablespoons yuzukosho
1 teaspoon grated fresh ginger

1 butter lettuce, torn
40 red shiso leaves
2 avocados

This is my favourite simple side salad. Yuzukosho pepper is the secret ingredient here — its limey peppery base is whisked with olive oil to make an intriguingly delicious dressing. Everyone always wants to know what gives it 'that special flavour'. Yuzukosho lasts forever in the fridge and is well worth seeking out and buying — I promise it won't be like that jar of preserved lemons you bought in 2006 that sat in the cupboard for five years.

To make the dressing, whisk together the oil, vinegar, yuzukosho and ginger.

Toss together the butter lettuce and shiso leaves with half the dressing and season to taste with salt and pepper.

Arrange the lettuce and shiso leaves around the edge of the salad bowl, leaving a well in the middle. Spoon the avocado into the well and finish with the remaining dressing.

Pasta salad with peas, broad beans & ricotta

Serves 4

200g peas, fresh or frozen

200g broad beans, fresh or frozen, skins removed if fresh

125ml olive oil

2 garlic cloves, finely chopped

Zest of 1 lemon

1 large handful basil leaves

1 handful mint leaves

400g rigatoni pasta

200g ricotta

Freshly grated Pecorino Romano, to serve

When I was young, the standard fare at any salad bar was a pasta salad, coleslaw, a rice salad and tinned beetroot. I still have a lot of affection for them all. This all-in-one carbs and vegies dish has a simple flavour profile that makes it perfect to serve with a wide range of meats, fish, chicken — maybe at a barbecue. I double-podded the broad beans here, but if I know my guests well, I won't be standing on such ceremony. You'll know you're a close friend when you find the bean skins!

Cook the peas and broad beans in boiling salted water for 4 minutes, or until quite soft. Drain, refresh under cold water and tip into a large bowl.

Crush the peas and beans with a potato masher or the back of a fork and season with sea salt and freshly ground black pepper. Stir in the olive oil, garlic, lemon zest, basil and mint.

Cook the pasta until al dente, following the packet instructions. Drain and toss with the peas and beans. Serve immediately, with spoonfuls of ricotta and a good grating of Pecorino and black pepper.

Warm spiced salad of pumpkin & cavolo nero with honey, tamari & toasted hazelnuts

Serves 4

2 tablespoons hazelnuts

1kg pumpkin or butternut squash, unpeeled, halved and deseeded

Olive oil, to drizzle

2 teaspoons smoked paprika

1 teaspoon chilli flakes

1 teaspoon ground cumin

1 teaspoon sea salt

1 bunch cavolo nero, stalks removed, leaves shredded

2 tablespoons tamari

1 tablespoon balsamic vinegar

1 tablespoon runny honey

Roast pumpkin is to Australians what roast potatoes are to the Brits. It is unsettling to move to another country and discover your favourite food is undervalued, undereaten and routinely fed to farm animals! This recipe is my secret plan to convert everyone to the absolute deliciousness of the humble Aussie roast pumpkin — I don't think it will be difficult.

Preheat the oven to 200°C. Line an oven tray with baking paper, scatter the hazelnuts on the tray and roast for 10–15 minutes. While still warm, tip into a tea towel and rub to remove the skins. Chop roughly.

Meanwhile, slice the pumpkin into thin wedges, leaving the skin on, and put in a large bowl. Drizzle with olive oil, sprinkle with smoked paprika, chilli flakes and ground cumin and mix well to coat. Spread out on 2 large baking trays and season with the sea salt. Roast for 10–15 minutes.

Remove the pumpkin from the oven and stir in the shredded cavolo nero. Return to the oven and cook for 15 minutes, until the pumpkin is golden and cooked through.

Stir well and drizzle with the tamari, balsamic vinegar and honey. Stir again and tip onto a serving platter. Scatter with the toasted hazelnuts.

Chopped salad with whipped ricotta

Serves 6–8

750g ricotta

250g Greek yoghurt

650g mixed tomatoes, small ones halved, larger ones cut into chunks

3 tablespoons extra virgin olive oil, plus extra to drizzle

1 garlic clove, crushed

½ red chilli, deseeded and finely chopped

1 teaspoon dried oregano

4 Lebanese cucumbers, chopped

200g radishes, chopped

1 handful dill, chopped

1 handful basil

You can't go wrong with this salad. It's refreshing and full of vibrant colours and textures — perfect for serving with barbecued meat or fish. Alternatively, enjoy it just as it is for lunch, with crusty bread for mopping up the whipped ricotta.

Beat the ricotta and yoghurt until smooth and season with sea salt.

Put the tomatoes in a large bowl. Add the olive oil, garlic, chilli and dried oregano and season well. Toss together and leave for 10 minutes.

To serve, spread the whipped ricotta over a serving platter. Top with the tomato salad, then add the cucumbers, radishes and herbs and dress with a little more olive oil.

Small Plates

Beef carpaccio with umeboshi & beetroot relish

Serves 4

250g rump steak
1 tablespoon light-flavoured oil
4 shiso leaves, finely shredded
1 tablespoon grated fresh horseradish
**2 tablespoons extra virgin olive oil,
to drizzle**

Umeboshi & beetroot relish

**300g beetroot, cooked, peeled and
roughly chopped**
1–2 tablespoons extra virgin olive oil
1 tablespoon grated fresh horseradish
30g umeboshi plums

*This carpaccio, with its tangy relish, is a very easy
and classic way to serve some lean meat; add a
platter of salad leaves and great bread and you're
good to go.*

Season the steak with lots of salt and pepper. Heat the oil in
a frying pan over high heat until smoking hot. Sear the steak
briefly on all sides until golden brown but not cooked
through. Transfer to a chopping board.

Cut the steak into 1cm thick slices. Lightly oil a piece of
baking paper and lay the slices on top. Fold the paper over
to cover the steak. Use a rolling pin to pound the steak into
very thin, wide slices.

To make the umeboshi & beetroot relish, blend or process
all the ingredients together into a rough paste.

Arrange the beef slices on a platter. Spoon a little relish over
the top, then sprinkle with shredded shiso and horseradish.
Finish with a scattering of sea salt and a drizzle of oil.

Tip

If you are not serving the steak straightaway, keep it wrapped
in paper in an airtight container in the fridge for 8 hours.

Umeboshi plums are salted plums, served in Japan as a
pickle. Look for them in Asian grocery stores. The umeboshi
& beetroot relish will make enough for a few servings; keep
it in an airtight container in the fridge for 5 days.

Chicken & black bean dumplings

Makes 30

Dumplings

50g fermented black beans
500g chicken mince
30g spring onions, finely chopped
20g chives, finely chopped
50ml soy sauce
25ml oyster sauce
25ml Shaoxing wine (Chinese cooking wine)
1 tablespoon black rice vinegar
30 wonton wrappers
2 tablespoons light-flavoured oil

Dipping sauce

30g fermented black beans
60g soft brown sugar
50ml soy sauce
2 teaspoons black rice vinegar
1 teaspoon Chinese five-spice
1 teaspoon Maggi seasoning, optional

As a nation, Australia has embraced the dumpling. My kids are obsessed with potstickers and gyoza and spent an entire summer, while we were working in Tokyo, on gyoza adventures – seeking out the best dumplings and rating them in a special holiday dumpling diary. This is one of their favourite flavour combinations. And if you too become a dumpling fanatic, you can buy a little plastic 'folding machine' to use at home. I would never call that cheating.

To make the dipping sauce, soak the beans in cold water for 10 minutes, then drain well. Combine all the ingredients with 100ml water in a small saucepan. Bring just to the boil, then reduce the heat and simmer for 10 minutes. Cool slightly, then blend until smooth. Pass through a fine sieve.

For the dumplings, soak the beans in cold water for 10 minutes, then drain well. Place the chicken mince, black beans, spring onion, chives, sauces, wine and vinegar in a large bowl. Mix together well with your hands.

Working with a few at a time, lay the wonton wrappers on a work surface and brush a little water around the edges. Place level tablespoons of filling in the centre and bring the opposite sides of the wrapper together to enclose. Work around the edge in a circle, pinching together to make a crescent-shaped parcel.

Heat the oil in a large frying pan over medium heat. Add the dumplings (you might need to cook in batches, depending on the size of your pan) and cook for 2 minutes, until the bases are golden and crispy. Add 5mm water to the pan, cover with a tight-fitting lid, reduce the heat to low and steam for 5 minutes, or until cooked through. Serve with the dipping sauce.

Roast cauliflower with pomegranate, ajo blanco & curry leaf oil

Serves 4

Ajo blanco

50g marcona almonds
50g peeled cucumber, roughly chopped
35ml olive oil
3 teaspoons sherry vinegar
1 garlic clove, crushed

Curry leaf oil

60ml olive oil
8 curry leaves
1 large pinch fenugreek seeds
1 large pinch yellow mustard seeds

650g cauliflower, broccoli or romanesco broccoli, broken into florets
2 tablespoons lemon juice
2 tablespoons extra virgin olive oil
120g pomegranate seeds
Ground sumac, to serve

We've certainly come a long way since the platters of party franks and cheese cubes on toothpicks. You can use cauliflower, broccoli or romanesco here – whatever's best and in season. And you can turn it into more of a salad by having less dip and piling up the roast vegies. If you're having guests and being organised, prebake the cauliflower and then just throw it in the oven for a few minutes to warm through.

To make the ajo blanco, put the almonds, cucumber, olive oil, sherry vinegar and garlic in a jug and mix with a stick blender until smooth and glossy. Season well.

To make the curry leaf oil, put the oil, curry leaves, fenugreek and mustard seeds in a small saucepan over low heat and bring to a simmer. Once the curry leaves have darkened and crisped, remove from the heat to cool.

Meanwhile, preheat the oven to 220°C. Spread the cauliflower on an oiled baking tray. Season and roast for 5–6 minutes until golden brown and tender.

Whisk together the lemon juice and olive oil to make a dressing and toss with the roast cauliflower.

Spoon the ajo blanco onto plates and pile the cauliflower on the sauce. Spoon pomegranate seeds over the top and drizzle with the curry leaf oil. Sprinkle with a pinch of sumac.

Tip

You can keep the ajo blanco in an airtight container in the fridge for up to 2 days, and the curry leaf oil in an airtight container in the pantry for up to 3 days.

Cold-drip negroni

Serves 1

30ml shiraz gin
20ml dry red vermouth
15ml campari
15ml cold-drip coffee
5ml cointreau
Ice cubes
1 strip orange peel, to garnish

Pour the gin, vermouth, campari, coffee and cointreau into a rocks glass of ice cubes and stir gently. Garnish with a twist of orange peel.

Negroni spritz

Serves 1

30ml campari
30ml rosso vermouth
Ice cubes
100ml sparkling wine
1 strip orange peel, to garnish

Add the campari and vermouth to a large wine glass of ice cubes and stir to combine. Add the sparkling wine and gently stir again. Garnish with a twist of orange peel.

Tokyo gimlet

Serves 1

45ml gin
25ml sake
15ml white sugar syrup
15ml fresh lime juice
2.5ml lime cordial
Ice cubes
Slice of lime, to garnish

Put the gin, sake, sugar syrup, lime juice, cordial and ice in a cocktail shaker and shake hard until frosty on the outside. Double strain into a chilled coupe glass. Garnish with a lime slice.

Tip

To make white sugar syrup, mix 220g caster sugar with 250ml water in a pan, bring to the boil and then reduce the heat to simmer for 3 minutes until dissolved. Cool and store in the fridge for up to 1 month.

Passionfruit caipiroska

Serves 1

Pulp of 1 passionfruit
4 lime wedges
15ml brown sugar syrup
50ml vodka
175g crushed ice

Muddle together the passionfruit, lime wedges and brown sugar syrup. Add the vodka and around 75g crushed ice and shake gently. Pour into a glass and top up with more crushed ice.

Tip

To make brown sugar syrup, mix 220g soft brown sugar with 250ml water in a pan, bring to the boil and then reduce the heat to simmer for 3 minutes until dissolved. Cool and store in the fridge for up to 1 month.

Clockwise from top: Tokyo gimlet; Negroni spritz;
Passionfruit caipiroska; Cold-drip negroni

Smashed cucumber with soy, peanut & miso dip

Serves 4

Soy, peanut and miso dip

300g silken tofu
2 tablespoons miso paste
2 tablespoons smooth peanut butter
2 teaspoons rice wine vinegar
2 teaspoons mirin
2 teaspoons olive oil

1 tablespoon soy yoghurt
1 tablespoon rice wine vinegar
1 teaspoon sesame oil
1 teaspoon tamari
1 tablespoon sugar
½ red chilli, finely sliced
1 cucumber
2 tablespoons unsalted roasted peanuts, roughly chopped
1 teaspoon black sesame seeds, toasted
Coriander cress, to serve

This is a dip to serve with crackers or, alternatively, just leave people to scoop it into small bowls and eat as it is. It's a healthy idea for nibbles and a great mix of textures — brilliant if you are inviting fashionably no-carb friends over for drinks.

To make the dip, blend all the ingredients together until smooth, then season to taste. Cover and refrigerate.

Stir together the yoghurt, vinegar, sesame oil, tamari and sugar with the chilli and a pinch of salt.

Top and tail the cucumber, then bash it gently along its length with a rolling pin. Quarter the cucumber lengthways, then chop into smaller pieces. Marinate the cucumber in the yoghurt mixture for 5–10 minutes.

Spoon the dip onto a plate and arrange the marinated cucumber and chilli on top. Garnish with peanuts, sesame seeds and coriander cress.

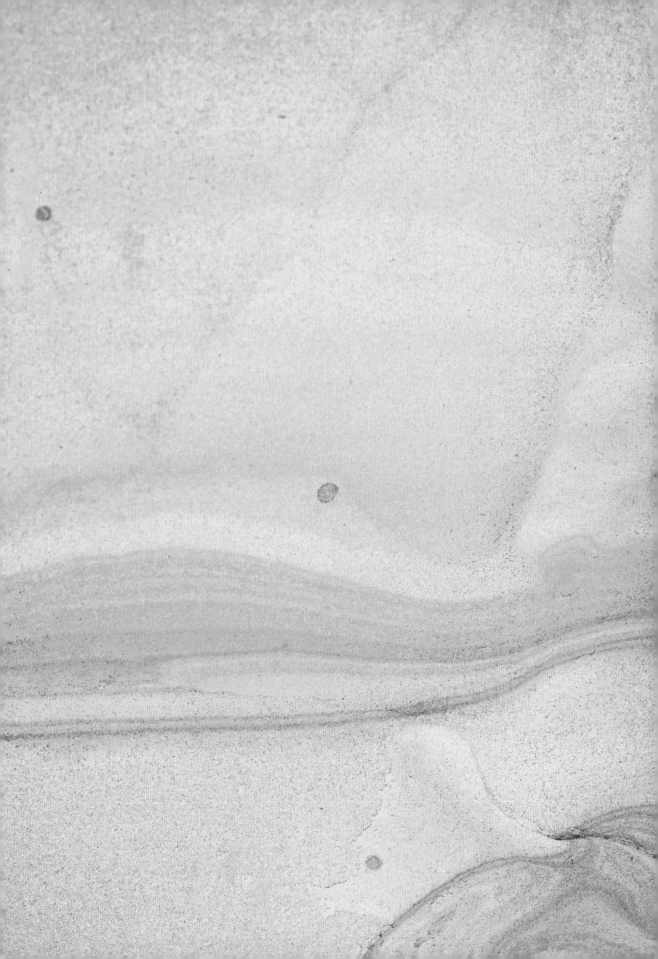

Barramundi crudo with avocado in dill & green tomato oil

Serves 4

Dill & green tomato oil

3 tablespoons olive oil
50g green tomato, roughly chopped
1 handful dill sprigs

2 avocados, roughly mashed
320g very fresh raw barramundi, skin removed, pin-boned and finely sliced
Zest and juice of 1 lemon
8 shiso leaves, finely sliced
20 baby spinach leaves, finely sliced
4 sorrel leaves, finely sliced
1 tablespoon olive oil

Crudo, sashimi, ceviche, poke — who would have thought raw fish, in all its guises, would become so popular? We always have one sort on the menu. Barramundi is an Australian favourite, but snapper, tuna or salmon would work equally well. This is the time to visit your trusted fishmonger — freshest is definitely best.

To make the dill & green tomato oil, mix the ingredients in a blender until smooth. Season to taste.

Mash the avocado into the dill & green tomato oil, season to taste and spoon over 4 plates (the oil will seep out a little). Lay the slices of fish on top and drizzle with lemon juice.

Mix the sliced shiso, spinach and sorrel leaves with the olive oil and a little lemon juice. Arrange on top of the fish. Finish with lemon zest to serve.

Tip

You can store the dill & green tomato oil in an airtight container in the fridge for up to 3 days.

Chilli, sesame & peanut crispy chicken with miso buttermilk dipping sauce

Serves 4

2 teaspoons salt

250ml buttermilk

4 skinless, boneless chicken thighs, each cut into 3 pieces

Light-flavoured oil, for deep-frying

90g rice flour

75g cornflour

2 tablespoons toasted peanuts, crushed

2 tablespoons sesame seeds

1 iceberg lettuce, leaves separated, to serve

Lime wedges, to serve

Gochujang sauce

30ml peanut oil

20g fresh ginger, peeled and finely grated

2 garlic cloves, crushed

150g Korean chilli bean paste (gochujang)

50ml mirin

2 tablespoons runny honey

2 tablespoons rice wine vinegar

30g soft brown sugar

Miso buttermilk dipping sauce

100ml buttermilk

25g miso paste

½ teaspoon dried aonori flakes

This dish inspires devotion like no other in the restaurants. I have had people stop me in the street to tell me how obsessed they are with it. It can also be served as a full meal, with a slaw made from crisp julienned kohlrabi, white cabbage and nashi pear mixed with coriander and mint leaves and dressed with olive oil and lime juice.

Dissolve the salt in 100ml water and mix with the buttermilk in a non-reactive dish. Add the chicken and turn to coat and completely cover in marinade. Cover and refrigerate for at least 2 hours (and up to 3 days).

To make the gochujang sauce, combine the oil, ginger and garlic in a small pan. Cook over low heat for about 3 minutes, until soft and fragrant. Stir in the remaining ingredients and simmer for 10 minutes until thick and sticky.

To make the miso buttermilk dipping sauce, stir together the buttermilk, miso and aonori and season to taste.

Half-fill a large heavy-based saucepan with oil and heat over medium–high heat to 180°C. Combine the rice flour and cornflour in a shallow dish. Working with a few pieces at a time, remove the chicken from the buttermilk marinade and shake off any excess liquid. Lightly dredge in the flours to coat, and shake off the excess.

Deep-fry the chicken in batches for 6–8 minutes until golden and crispy. Remove with a slotted spoon and drain on kitchen paper. Keep warm while you cook the rest.

Toss the fried chicken in the warm gochujang sauce, pile on a platter and scatter with toasted peanuts and sesame. Serve with lettuce leaves, lime wedges and miso buttermilk dipping sauce.

Kimchi, spinach & ricotta dumplings

Makes 44

Dashi

70g kombu
30g bonito flakes

Dumplings

2 large bunches spinach, stalks trimmed
250g kimchi, drained, chopped
2 spring onions, chopped
60g fresh ricotta, gently crumbled
44 wonton wrappers
1 egg, lightly beaten
Chilli oil, to serve

I've always adored the sour–sweet tang of pickles and sauerkraut, long before we all discovered their links to great gut health. Even as a child, I loved little pickled onions from a jar (although I'm not entirely sure of their implications for gut health). In more recent times, Australia has discovered the joy of kimchi. I was so excited when I got the opportunity to open a restaurant in Korea. I flew out there one January, into the freezing cold, and ate bags of hot dumplings filled with new flavours and textures. This recipe is based on Korean kimchi mandu, but using the Western favourite, ricotta. It is a strange-sounding combination that really works. This recipe makes a good big batch of dumplings — you can freeze them, filled but uncooked, for up to 1 month.

For the dashi, combine the kombu and 1.25 litres water in a saucepan. Simmer, partially covered, over low heat for 20 minutes, then add the bonito flakes and simmer for a further 5 minutes. Leave to cool, then strain.

To make the dumplings, put the spinach in a large heatproof bowl and cover with boiling water. Leave for 30 seconds, then drain and plunge into iced water. Leave for 30 seconds, then drain and squeeze out all the water. Weigh out 80g of the spinach. Chop and separate it so it doesn't clump.

Gently mix the spinach with the kimchi, spring onions and ricotta, without breaking up the ricotta too much.

Working with a few at a time, lay the wonton wrappers on a work surface and brush a little beaten egg around the edges. Place 1 heaped teaspoon of filling in the centre of each. Fold in half, removing any air pockets, and seal the edges by pinching together with your fingers.

Reheat the dashi in a pan and poach the dumplings in batches for 2 minutes. Lift out with a slotted spoon. Serve with a spoonful of dashi and a little chilli oil.

Watermelon & lime frappé

Serves 1

250g frozen watermelon flesh
30ml fresh lime juice
15ml agave syrup

Place all the ingredients in a blender with
100ml water and blend until smooth. Serve
in a tall glass.

Cold-drip espresso martini

Serves 1

45ml vodka
45ml cold-drip coffee
25ml brown sugar syrup (see page 174)
15ml coffee liqueur
Ice cubes
3 coffee beans, to garnish

Place all the ingredients except the coffee beans
in a cocktail shaker. Shake hard and strain into a
chilled coupe glass. Garnish with the coffee beans.

Plum & cardamom shrub

Serves 1

Plum shrub (makes 6 drinks)
500g plums, thinly sliced and pitted
150g sugar
½ teaspoon ground cardamom
½ teaspoon crushed black peppercorns
200ml apple cider vinegar

45ml gold rum
75ml plum shrub, above
1 teaspoon fresh lime juice
Ice cubes
50ml soda water

To make the plum shrub, mix the plums, sugar
and spices in an airtight container in the fridge.
Stir every day for 4 days. Strain the plums out of
the liquid, and stir the vinegar into the liquid.
Return the plums to the liquid. Cover and return
to the fridge for 1–2 days. Strain the liquid – this
is the plum shrub – keeping the plums to garnish.
Will keep in the fridge for up to 1 week.

Pour the rum, plum shrub and lime juice into a
large glass and stir well. Add the ice cubes and
top up with soda. Garnish with pickled plum.

Dark & stormy

Serves 1

Ginger syrup
250g caster sugar
100g grated fresh ginger
6 cardamom pods, crushed
2 cloves
8g peppercorns

45ml black rum
15ml fresh lime juice
30ml ginger syrup, above
Ice cubes
90ml soda water
1 lime slice, to garnish

To make the ginger syrup, put all the ingredients
in a small pan with 400ml water and bring to
the boil, then simmer for 20 minutes. Cool and
strain well. Keep in the fridge for up to 2 weeks.

Add the rum, lime juice, ginger syrup and ice to
a rocks glass. Top up with soda and a lime slice.

**Clockwise from top: Cold-drip espresso martini;
Plum & cardamom shrub; Dark & stormy;
Watermelon & lime frappé**

Whipped avocado & tofu with chia & seaweed crackers

Serves 4–6

Chia & seaweed crackers

50g chia seeds
40g ground linseeds
35g sesame seeds
½ nori sheet, crumbled or chopped into small pieces
½ teaspoon tamari
¼ teaspoon salt

Whipped avocado & tofu

100g firm silken tofu
Juice of 1 lime
2 avocados
2 spring onions, chopped
1 small handful coriander, chopped
1 small handful parsley, chopped
½ long green chilli, deseeded and chopped

To serve

12 small endive leaves
100g radishes, finely sliced
¼ cucumber, quartered lengthways
1 tablespoon chopped coriander
1 tablespoon finely sliced spring onions
½ long green chilli, deseeded and finely sliced

When a commentator in The Australian *newspaper declared that millennials can't afford to buy their own homes because they spend too much money on avocado toast in cafés, politics and food culture collided in a way the world hadn't seen since Marie Antoinette and her cake. With this recipe, you can have your avocado as a healthy dip that goes a long way, and still save up for that house.*

The crackers have a Nordic feel, with their crunchy seeds and salty seaweed hint. I think they're perfect with the creaminess of the avocado.

To make the crackers, preheat the oven to 170°C. Combine the chia, linseeds, sesame, nori, tamari and salt in a bowl. Add 125ml water and use a silicone spatula to mix thoroughly. Set aside for 10 minutes.

Lay out a sheet of baking paper and place the dough onto it. Press out until about 1cm thick, then place another sheet of baking paper on top. Roll with a rolling pin until 2mm thick. Make sure it is even, and not thicker in the middle.

Remove the top sheet of paper and lift the dough on the paper onto a large baking tray. Bake for 30 minutes and then remove from the oven (but leave the oven on).

Cool slightly, then break into 16 roughly even-sized pieces. Return to the baking tray, turning the crackers upside down. Cook for a further 15 minutes, or until crisp. Transfer to a wire rack to cool completely.

For the whipped avocado & tofu, mix the tofu and lime juice in a food processor until almost smooth. Add the avocados and blend again until smooth. Add the spring onion, herbs and chilli and mix with the pulse button, leaving specks of green in the mixture. Season with salt.

Spoon the whipped avocado onto plates and add the endive leaves, radishes and cucumber. Sprinkle with chopped coriander, spring onion and chilli, and serve with the chia & seaweed crackers.

Zucchini fries with tahini yoghurt dip

Serves 4

Tahini yoghurt dip

2 tablespoons tahini
3 tablespoons lemon juice
½ garlic clove, finely chopped
250g Greek yoghurt
1 tablespoon olive oil
1 teaspoon sea salt
10g nigella seeds, lightly toasted

Zucchini fries

4 zucchini (courgettes)
125g semolina
25g cornflour
125ml milk
Light-flavoured oil, for deep-frying
Lemon wedges, to serve

I'd be very happy to eat a plate of these with a glass of wine for dinner. I have never forgotten something Joanna Lumley once said about her ideal dinner being a glass of champagne and a crisp — I do need a few more food groups, but I'm with you in spirit, Joanna. After a long working day, a special treat is to sit in the restaurant and enjoy these with a few olives and a drink — and I'm done. These are incredibly easy to make if you're having friends around — shallow-fry them if you don't have a deep fryer (it will just take a little longer). Serve with a couple of other dishes or maybe a cheese platter.

To make the tahini yoghurt dip, put the tahini in a bowl and squeeze the lemon juice over it — it will seize. Mix in the garlic, then add the yoghurt, olive oil and salt and beat until combined. Stir in the nigella seeds.

Finely slice the zucchini about 5mm thick, using a mandoline if you have one.

Mix together the semolina and cornflour in a shallow bowl. Put the milk in another shallow bowl.

Heat the oil in a large pan or deep fryer to 180°C. Dip the zucchini in the milk, then press in the semolina coating, turning to coat all sides. Deep-fry the zucchini for around 5 minutes, or until lightly golden and crisp.

Scatter the fries with sea salt and serve with the tahini yoghurt dip and lemon wedges.

Barbecue

Beef bavette with herb & peanut relish

Serves 4

1 red chilli, chopped
1 garlic clove, sliced
1 tablespoon runny honey
2 tablespoons soy sauce
2 tablespoons rice wine vinegar
Juice of 1 lime
750g beef bavette (skirt), or onglet

Herb & peanut relish

2 teaspoons caster sugar
Juice of 2 limes
2 tablespoons fish sauce
2 teaspoons soy sauce
1cm piece fresh ginger, peeled and grated
1 garlic clove, grated
45g toasted unsalted peanuts, chopped
1 tablespoon chopped coriander leaves
1 French shallot, finely sliced
2 red chillies, chopped

Pickled cucumber

1 teaspoon caster sugar
2 tablespoons rice wine vinegar
½ cucumber, cut into chunks

When I was a little boy Dad would bring bavette and lamb shanks home for the dog because nobody wanted to buy them. Oh, to be a butcher's dog! Bavette, like lamb shanks, has since been discovered as a great cut of meat (and the price has gone up accordingly). It's not a tender cut, but not all meat has to be. As a wise Italian chef once told me, it's about 'enjoying the chew'.

Combine the chilli, garlic, honey, soy sauce, vinegar and lime juice in a shallow non-reactive dish. Add the beef, toss well and leave to marinate for at least 30 minutes, or ideally overnight in the fridge.

To make the herb & peanut relish, mix together all the ingredients. Check the seasoning.

To make the pickled cucumber, mix together the sugar and rice wine vinegar in a bowl and season well with salt. Add the cucumber and leave for 10 minutes.

Heat your barbecue until hot and ready to cook on. Remove the beef from its marinade, pat dry and season with salt. Barbecue for 4–5 minutes on each side, or until nicely charred but still springy to the touch.

Transfer the beef to a board, cover loosely with foil and leave to rest for 10 minutes. Cut into thick slices and serve with the herb & peanut relish and pickled cucumber.

Paprika lamb skewers with capsicum & parsley salad

Serves 4

2 tablespoons olive oil
1 teaspoon paprika
1 tablespoon maple syrup
2 tablespoons soy sauce
1 teaspoon ground cumin
¼ teaspoon crushed Szechuan peppercorns or pepper
1 small onion, grated
½ teaspoon chilli flakes
600g lamb backstrap or fillet, cut into 2cm cubes
8–10 fresh bay leaves

Capsicum & parsley salad

2 grilled red capsicums (peppers), from a jar or the barbecue, thickly sliced
1 large handful flat-leaf parsley
Juice of ½ lemon
1½ tablespoons olive oil

To serve

150g Greek yoghurt
2 garlic cloves, crushed
1 lemon, cut into wedges

Cubes of pork shoulder or chicken would work just as well on the skewers here. As you've got the barbie fired up, you could use it to gently sweat the fresh capsicums (red peppers) for the salad, or keep things quick and easy and use the ones from a jar, as I've done here. If you're having friends over, make a big batch of these and serve with plain warm flatbreads (page 108).

Mix together the olive oil, paprika, maple syrup, soy sauce, cumin, peppercorns, onion and chilli in a bowl and add the cubes of lamb. Cover and set aside to marinate for 15 minutes. Thread the lamb onto metal or soaked wooden skewers with a couple of bay leaves between the lamb cubes.

Heat your barbecue until hot and ready to cook on. Cook the skewers for around 8 minutes, turning until browned.

To make the capsicum & parsley salad, toss together all the ingredients and season with salt and ground black pepper.

To serve, combine the yoghurt and garlic in a small bowl and season with sea salt. Serve the skewers with the capsicum salad, garlic yoghurt and lemon wedges.

Spiced squid or sausage sizzle with burnt tomato & chilli salsa

Serves 4

1kg squid, cleaned and left whole, or 4 good-quality sausages
1 tablespoon olive oil, plus extra to drizzle
2 teaspoons chilli flakes
1 large handful rocket, to serve

Burnt tomato & chilli salsa

¼ red onion, finely chopped
5 tomatoes
2 red chillies
2 tablespoons olive oil
2 garlic cloves, crushed
1 teaspoon balsamic vinegar
1 small handful mint leaves, chopped

Get any group of Australians standing around chatting for long enough, and someone will wheel a barbecue into the middle and you've got yourself a sausage sizzle. As an Aussie in Britain, we do tend to get a little typecast. When our girls started primary school I was asked to help with the barbecue fundraiser. It was manned by one Brit and three Aussie dads and I was asked to come up with a relish accompaniment for the meat. It's become an annual favourite — I still do the barbecue, even though the kids have long since left primary school. Now I serve this to new keen-bean school parents, who make me feel very old!

Heat your barbecue until hot and ready to cook on.

Meanwhile, make the burnt tomato & chilli salsa. Put the onion in a bowl of cold water and set aside. Place the tomatoes and chilli on the barbecue grill and cook, turning occasionally, until they are blackened and soft — this will be about 6 minutes for the chillies and 10 minutes for the tomatoes. Peel the tomatoes and finely chop into a bowl. Peel the chillies, discarding the stem and skin, finely chop and add to the tomatoes. Add the drained onion, olive oil, garlic and vinegar and stir together. Season with sea salt, then fold in the mint.

Pat the squid dry with kitchen paper and toss in a bowl with the olive oil and chilli flakes. Barbecue the squid for 1–2 minutes on each side, until nicely charred. Remove from the barbecue and drizzle with a little olive oil. Or cook the sausages for 10–15 minutes, until cooked through.

Serve the squid or sausages with the rocket and the burnt tomato & chilli salsa.

Prawn burger with jalapeño mayo, pickled radishes & sesame gochujang

Serves 4

Prawn burgers

4cm piece fresh ginger, peeled and finely chopped

1 lemongrass stalk, white part only, bruised and finely chopped

1 small handful coriander

1 garlic clove, finely chopped

200g firm white fish, skin and bones removed

400g raw prawns, peeled and deveined

1 chilli, finely chopped

2 makrut lime leaves, finely chopped

Pickled radishes

1 tablespoon mustard seeds

100ml rice wine vinegar

30g icing sugar

1 teaspoon salt

1 bunch mixed radishes, finely sliced with a mandoline

Jalapeño mayo

1 tablespoon sliced jalapeños from a jar, roughly chopped

1 handful coriander leaves, chopped

125ml aioli

Juice of ½ lime

Gochujang sesame dressing

4 tablespoons Korean chilli bean paste (gochujang)

2 tablespoons rice wine vinegar

2 teaspoons runny honey

4 tablespoons toasted sesame seeds

1 tablespoon light-flavoured oil

4 brioche rolls, shop-bought or see recipe page 36

½ iceberg lettuce

1 bunch coriander

For a while there, the world (well, the American world) imagined that we ate grilled prawns for dinner every day in Australia because Crocodile Dundee told them he'd 'slip an extra shrimp on the barbie'. (For the record, shrimps are what the Americans call king prawns.) Here's my homage to that bit of Aussie popular culture. Slice the radish on a mandoline and leave it in the pickling liquid so it stays crisp while you barbecue the prawn burgers. If you don't have time to make the salad, serve with a little watercress.

Make the prawn burgers the day before you need them. Pulse the ginger, lemongrass, coriander and garlic in a food processor, add the white fish and a quarter of the prawns. Pulse until very finely chopped but not quite smooth. Roughly chop the remaining prawns into small pieces by hand and stir into the mixture with the chopped chilli and lime leaves. Season with salt and pepper.

With wet hands, divide the mix into 4 balls and shape into patties. Leave uncovered overnight in the fridge to dry out.

To make the pickled radishes, warm the mustard seeds in a saucepan over medium heat until they start to pop. Add the vinegar, sugar and salt and 200ml water and warm gently until dissolved. Remove from the heat, add the radishes and leave for 20 minutes to cool completely.

To make the jalapeño mayo, mix all the ingredients together, cover and leave in the fridge.

To make the gochujang sesame dressing, mix together the chilli paste, vinegar and honey and cover until needed. Stir in the sesame seeds just before serving.

Lightly brush the prawn burgers with oil. Heat your barbecue until hot and ready to cook on. Cook the burgers for 4 minutes on each side, then leave to rest for a few minutes before serving in lightly toasted brioche rolls. Add the jalapeño mayo, lettuce leaves, some coriander and pickled radishes to each burger. Serve the gochujang sesame dressing on the side.

Turmeric-spiced chicken in lettuce parcels with green chilli dipping sauce

Serves 4

Green chilli dipping sauce

60g palm sugar, crumbled or grated
5 green chillies, deseeded
1 green bird's eye chilli
Stalks from 1 small bunch coriander
10 mint leaves
2 garlic cloves, chopped
3cm piece fresh ginger, peeled and grated
185ml lime juice
3 tablespoons fish sauce

Turmeric-spiced chicken

2 tablespoons fish sauce
1 heaped teaspoon ground turmeric
2 makrut lime leaves
400ml tin coconut milk
1 lemongrass stalk, white part only, bruised and roughly chopped
1 banana shallot, chopped
2cm piece fresh ginger, peeled and grated
1 teaspoon sugar
8 chicken thighs, with skin

To serve

½ iceberg lettuce, cut into wedges
¼ red cabbage, finely sliced
¼ white cabbage, finely sliced
2 limes, cut into wedges
1 small bunch coriander
4 tablespoons peanuts
4 teaspoons crispy shallots

This is one of my favourite Aussie summer dishes — a great combination of barbecued spiced meat with fresh crisp leaves and a Thai-style dipping sauce. Shred the chicken and toss it through the sauce, then scoop it up in lettuce cups. Use fresh turmeric when you can get it (it's the newest anti-inflammatory superfood).

You can make the green chilli dipping sauce in advance and store it in the fridge. Gently melt the palm sugar in a pan, then cool slightly. Pound the chillies, coriander stalks, mint, garlic and ginger with a mortar and pestle or pulse in a food processor until finely chopped but not smooth. Mix with the palm sugar. Stir in the lime juice and fish sauce — the sauce should be sour, spicy and sweet.

To make the turmeric-spiced chicken, stir the fish sauce, turmeric, lime leaves, coconut milk, lemongrass, shallot, ginger and sugar together in a pan. Add the chicken, skin side down, and bring to a simmer. Cover and simmer for 20 minutes, or until the chicken is cooked through. Leave to cool in the poaching liquid.

Remove the chicken from the poaching liquid and pat dry. Simmer the poaching liquid over medium heat until reduced by half, to make a sauce.

Heat your barbecue until hot and ready to cook on. Grill the chicken on high heat, charring the skin. Roughly chop, then place in a bowl with the warm turmeric sauce and toss gently.

Serve the chicken with the lettuce leaves, cabbage, lime wedges, coriander, peanuts, crispy shallots and the green chilli dipping sauce.

Grilled octopus with pomegranate & parsley dressing

Serves 4

Red capsicum & walnut sauce

1 grilled red capsicum (pepper) from a jar, drained

2 garlic cloves, chopped

100g walnuts, toasted

Zest and juice of ½ lemon

2–3 tablespoons olive oil

1 teaspoon sweet smoked paprika

½ teaspoon ground cumin

½ teaspoon ground coriander

Pomegranate & parsley dressing

Seeds from ½ pomegranate

1 small handful parsley, chopped

2½ tablespoons olive oil

Zest and juice of ½ lemon

½ red onion, finely sliced

Octopus

600g cooked octopus legs (about 4 large or 6 medium)

Zest and juice of 1 orange

Juice of 1 lemon

5 bay leaves

1 teaspoon dried juniper berries

3 tablespoons olive oil

Because we have a vibrant Greek community with such a strong food culture, octopus is a beloved menu item in Australia. Even if we're not confident enough to prepare it at home, we love to eat it when we're out. If it's not something you've cooked on the barbecue before, you can now buy just the tentacles in an easy pack at the supermarket. No excuse!

You can make the red capsicum & walnut sauce in advance and keep it refrigerated in an airtight container for 2 days. Put all the ingredients in a blender and blitz to a thick paste.

To make the pomegranate & parsley dressing, mix together all the ingredients well and season to taste. Keep refrigerated in an airtight container until ready to use.

Marinate the octopus legs before barbecuing. Whisk together the orange zest and juice, lemon juice, bay leaves, juniper berries and olive oil in a pan over low heat. Simmer for 5 minutes, until slightly reduced, and then remove from the heat. Cool a little, then pour over the octopus legs and leave to marinate for 15 minutes.

Heat your barbecue until hot and ready to cook on. Grill the octopus legs for 3–4 minutes on each side, brushing with the marinade during cooking. The octopus should have char marks from the barbecue grill.

Serve the octopus with the red capsicum & walnut sauce and a generous drizzle of dressing.

Grilled pork chops & cashew satay with pineapple & cucumber relish

Serves 4

1 tablespoon sesame oil
1 tablespoon kecap manis
1 teaspoon ground cumin
1 teaspoon ground coriander
1 teaspoon ground turmeric
1 teaspoon agave syrup or sugar
1 lemongrass stalk, white part only, bruised and roughly chopped
1 garlic clove, crushed
2cm piece fresh ginger, peeled and grated
4 pork chops

Cashew satay

120g raw cashew nuts
125ml coconut milk
1 teaspoon ground cumin
1 teaspoon ground coriander
1 teaspoon turmeric
2 tablespoons kecap manis
1 teaspoon tamarind purée

Pineapple & cucumber relish

1 French shallot, finely chopped
1 Lebanese cucumber, diced
100g fresh pineapple, diced
½ teaspoon salt
2 tablespoons rice wine vinegar

This is an update of those exotic pork and pineapple dishes from the seventies. I think the Brits were responsible for that combination (they did have 150 years of food influence over Australia) and I hold up my experience of a slice of tinned pineapple on a gammon steak in evidence. This sour pineapple & cucumber relish paired with the sweet satay listens more to the influence of our Asian neighbours. This marinade would work brilliantly with chicken thighs too.

Mix together the sesame oil, kecap manis, cumin, coriander, turmeric, agave, lemongrass, garlic and ginger in a non-reactive dish to make a marinade. Add the pork chops, stir to coat and leave to marinate in the fridge for at least 12 hours.

To make the cashew satay, preheat the oven to 180°C and roast the cashew nuts on a baking tray for 8–10 minutes or until golden brown. While still warm, mix in a blender with the other ingredients to make a smooth sauce. Leave to cool and then store in an airtight container in the fridge if necessary until needed.

To make the pineapple & cucumber relish, stir together all the ingredients and keep in the fridge until needed.

Heat your barbecue until hot and ready to cook on. Lift the pork chops out of the marinade and cook for 5–7 minutes on each side until charred and cooked through. Leave to rest for a few minutes, then serve with the cashew satay and relish.

Miso roast beef fillet with ginger & spring onion dressing

Serves 4

1 tablespoon light-flavoured oil
2 tablespoons red or brown miso paste
600g beef eye fillet

Ginger & spring onion dressing

4 tablespoons light soy sauce
1 tablespoon sesame oil
2 tablespoons rice wine vinegar
1 garlic clove, crushed
2cm piece fresh ginger, peeled and grated
6 spring onions, finely chopped

To serve

Micro herbs
Cooked noodles

A whole beef fillet is an extravagance: I always gasp at the price. But it's very easy to cook, perfect for a barbecue and can be served at room temperature — an entertainer's dream. Wrap it in foil after cooking, while it rests, to keep it warm. Its luxeness is what makes it so special to share with friends. I serve this with noodles and lots of vegie sides.

Stir the oil into the miso. Pat the beef dry with kitchen paper, then rub with the miso oil. Marinate in the fridge for at least 2 hours, and up to 24 hours. Remove from the fridge to come to room temperature 30 minutes before cooking.

To make the ginger & spring onion dressing, whisk together the soy sauce, sesame oil, vinegar, garlic and ginger. Add the spring onions.

Heat your barbecue until hot and ready to cook on. Sear the beef fillet on each side for 4–6 minutes, then reduce the heat to medium and cook for a further 6–8 minutes, turning occasionally. Take off the heat, cover with foil and leave to rest before slicing.

Slice the beef fillet, spoon the dressing and any meat juices over the top and scatter with micro herbs. Delicious with noodles, with any extra dressing poured over the top.

Sticky chilli pork belly with barbecue sauce

Serves 4

Light-flavoured oil

600g pork belly, bone removed, cut into 3cm cubes

1 litre beef stock

1 red chilli

5 garlic cloves, peeled, left whole and lightly crushed

10cm piece fresh ginger, peeled and thinly sliced

2 spring onions, roughly chopped

1 tablespoon Chinese five-spice

125ml light soy sauce

1 tablespoon oyster sauce

125ml Shaoxing wine (Chinese cooking wine)

2 tablespoons caster sugar

Barbecue sauce

4 tablespoons Korean chilli bean paste (gochujang)

2 tablespoons runny honey

2cm piece fresh ginger, peeled and grated

2 tablespoons light soy sauce

1 tablespoon light-flavoured oil

Salad dressing

4 tablespoons red wine vinegar

2 tablespoons fish sauce

1½ tablespoons sesame oil

To serve

Crisp lettuce leaves

4 tablespoons peanuts

4 tablespoons crispy shallots

1 bunch each coriander and mint

2 spring onions, finely sliced

Pork belly has been the dish of the past decade. The secret is in slow cooking: you want to render all the fat out of the pork belly before barbecuing it to irresistible stickiness. Serve the pork belly with lettuce leaves to wrap it up in — a great barbecue tip that saves on cutlery!

Heat a large saucepan over medium–high heat. Drizzle a little oil into the pan and sear the pork belly on all sides until browned. Add the stock, chilli, garlic, ginger, spring onion, five-spice, soy sauce, oyster sauce, wine and sugar and bring to the boil. Reduce the heat to a high simmer and cover the pan with a lid.

Simmer the pork for 1 hour, then remove the lid and simmer for 30–45 minutes until the stock has completely reduced and is sticking to the meat, and the fat is starting to separate.

Meanwhile, to make the barbecue sauce, stir together all the ingredients in a bowl.

In another bowl, whisk together the ingredients for the salad dressing and set aside.

Remove the pork from the heat and stir into the barbecue sauce, thoroughly coating the pieces of pork belly.

Heat your barbecue until hot and ready to cook on. Chargrill the pork belly pieces on all sides until caramelised and just starting to char, brushing with extra sauce from the pan as you turn them.

Serve on a platter, with the lettuce, peanuts, crispy shallots, herbs and spring onions scattered over the top. Spoon the salad dressing over to serve.

Big Plates

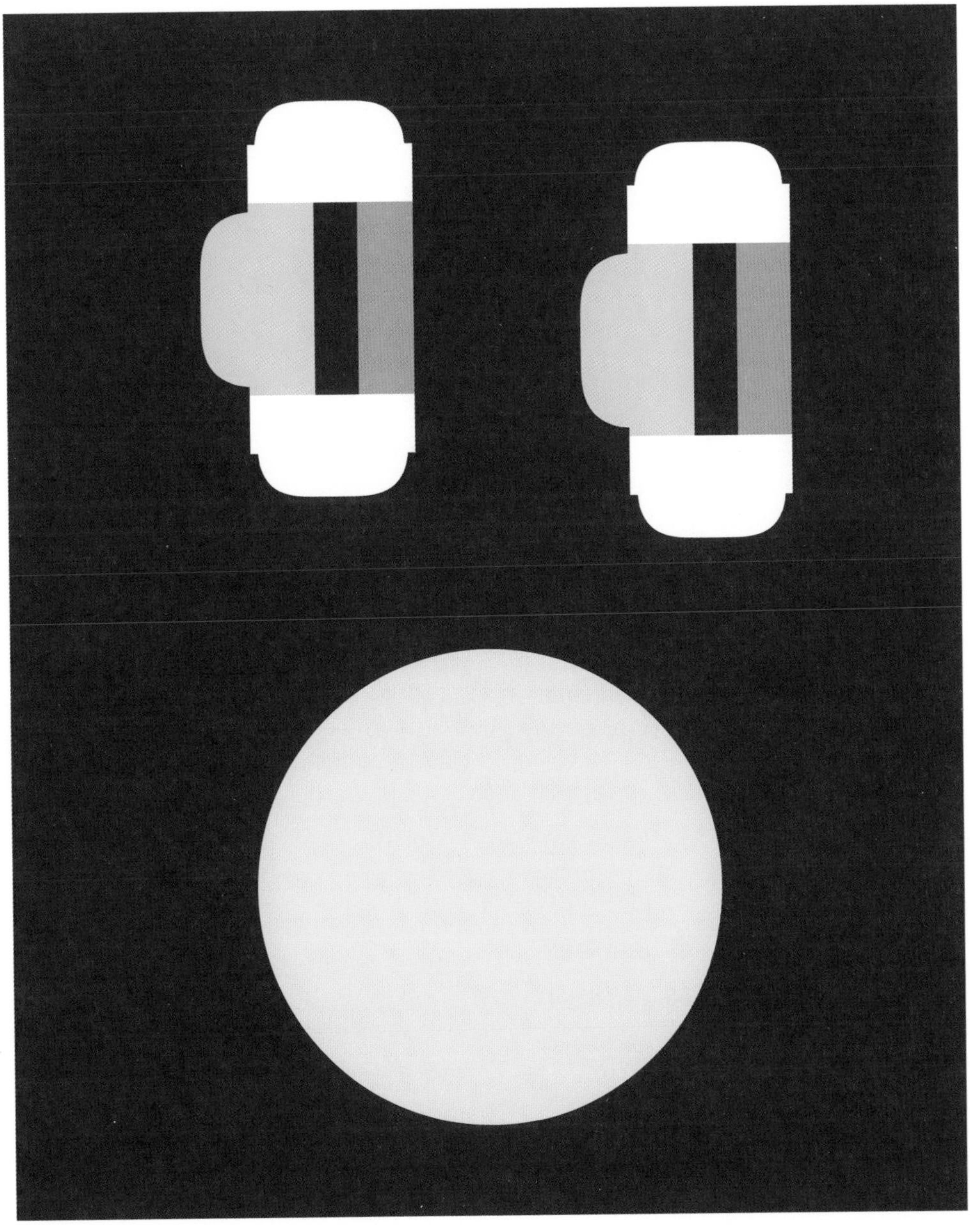

Lentil tacos with buffalo mozzarella & pickled red onion

Serves 4

Ancho-braised lentils

200g brown lentils
1 tablespoon olive oil
½ onion, finely diced
1 bay leaf
1 dried ancho chilli
½ cinnamon stick
1 handful coriander leaves, chopped
½ green chilli, finely chopped
2cm piece fresh ginger, peeled and finely chopped

Pickled red onion

1 tablespoon mustard seeds
100ml rice wine vinegar
30g icing sugar
1 teaspoon salt
1 red onion, finely sliced

To serve

12 soft tacos
2 avocados, mashed with a little salt and olive oil
250g buffalo mozzarella, torn into bite-sized pieces
1 handful coriander leaves
Zest of 1 lemon
4 tablespoons crispy shallots

I cook up loads of these lentils at a time and get a couple of meals out of them — they make the base of a very good lentil chilli, too. Use non-dairy cheese here and you've got a great meal for feeding the family vegan.

Rinse the lentils in a sieve until the water runs clear. Heat the olive oil in a pan over low heat, add the onion and cook until softened. Add the lentils, bay leaf, ancho chilli and cinnamon stick and cook, stirring, for 2 minutes. Add 500ml water and bring to a simmer.

Simmer the lentils for 35–40 minutes until very soft, stirring occasionally and adding more water if needed. The lentils should be mashable. Remove from the heat and stir in the coriander, green chilli and ginger. Season with salt.

Meanwhile, to make the pickled red onion, warm the mustard seeds in a saucepan over medium heat until they start to pop. Add the vinegar, sugar and salt and 200ml water and warm gently until dissolved. Remove from the heat and pour over the sliced onion. This can be used immediately, or left to pickle for a while.

Serve each taco with a heaped tablespoon of lentils, mashed avocado, mozzarella and pickled red onion. Scatter with coriander, lemon zest and crispy shallots.

Green chicken, eggplant & green bean curry

Serves 4

Thai green curry paste

1 teaspoon white peppercorns
1 teaspoon coriander seeds
½ teaspoon cumin seeds
1 teaspoon salt
1 teaspoon ground turmeric
1 lemongrass stalk, white part only, bruised and roughly chopped
6 garlic cloves, chopped
4 spring onions, chopped
2 tablespoons coriander stalks, chopped
3cm piece fresh ginger, peeled and chopped
4 green chillies, deseeded and chopped
2 tablespoons light-flavoured oil

Chicken curry

1 tablespoon light-flavoured oil
125ml chicken stock
250ml coconut milk
1 anchovy, finely chopped
4 makrut lime leaves, torn, or 3 strips lime peel
500g skinless chicken breast fillets, cut into chunks
100g green beans, halved lengthways
1 handful baby corn
400g eggplant (aubergine), cut into chunks
1 tablespoon caster sugar
2 tablespoons fish sauce
1 tablespoon lime juice
1 handful basil leaves
3 green chillies, deseeded and sliced
Steamed rice, to serve

Sydney's Thai Town doesn't rival its Chinatown for size, but it packs quite a flavour punch. It's a rite of passage for young Aussies to travel through Asia and as a nation we've embraced the Thai curry in the same way the Brits embraced chicken tikka masala. If you're wondering what on earth the anchovy is doing in here, the traditional Thai green curry wraps dried shrimp paste in foil and then burns it over a flame. I always feel like an embarrassing extra in Breaking Bad *when I try to do that — the anchovy gives the same umami punch, without the theatrics.*

To make the Thai green curry paste, heat a small pan over medium heat. Add the peppercorns, coriander and cumin seeds and toast for 1–2 minutes or until fragrant. Put the toasted spices and remaining ingredients in a food processor and pulse to a paste, scraping down the side of the bowl occasionally. You will need 3 tablespoons of the paste for a curry to serve 4. You can save leftover paste in an airtight container in the fridge for a couple of weeks.

To make the curry, heat a large saucepan over high heat. Add the oil and 3 tablespoons curry paste and cook for 2 minutes or until fragrant. Add the stock, coconut milk, anchovy and lime leaves, reduce the heat and simmer for 5 minutes.

Add the chicken to the pan and cook for a further 5 minutes. Stir in the beans, baby corn, eggplant, sugar, fish sauce and lime juice and cook for 5 minutes.

Scatter with the basil leaves and chilli and serve with steamed rice.

Spiced meatballs with eggs, red capsicum & tomato

Serves 4

300g lamb mince

½ onion, finely chopped

2 garlic cloves, crushed

1 large handful fresh breadcrumbs

1 teaspoon ground cinnamon

1 handful parsley leaves, roughly chopped

2 tablespoons olive oil

400g tin chopped tomatoes

2 grilled red capsicums (peppers) from a jar, torn

1 teaspoon caster sugar

1 tablespoon harissa

4 eggs

1 teaspoon ground sumac

Pitta or flatbreads (page 108), to serve

This is a favourite weeknight dinner that doubles as a great winter brunch if you're having friends over. The flavours are a lovely combination of Italian meatballs with a hint of shakshuka, the Israeli egg dish that is one of my most-loved breakfasts.

If you're well organised, make a double batch of the meatballs and stash half of them in the freezer.

Put the mince in a large bowl with the onion, garlic and breadcrumbs. Add the cinnamon and parsley and season with salt and freshly ground black pepper. Use your hands to squeeze together until well combined. Wet your hands and roll the mixture into 12 small meatballs.

Heat the oil in a large heavy-based frying pan over medium–high heat. Fry the meatballs for 6–8 minutes, turning frequently, until golden brown.

Add the chopped tomatoes, capsicum, sugar and harissa and simmer until the sauce has thickened and the meatballs are cooked through. Season to taste.

Use a wooden spoon to make 4 holes in the tomato sauce in the pan and break an egg into each hole. Cook until the egg whites have set but the yolks are still runny. Sprinkle with sumac and serve with the breads.

Chilli miso salmon with hot & sour eggplant

Serves 4

4 tablespoons sugar

4 tablespoons mirin

2 tablespoons sake

6 tablespoons white miso paste

2 tablespoons Korean chilli bean paste (gochujang)

4 x 150g pieces skinless salmon fillet

100g frozen edamame beans

1 small handful pea shoots

1 handful coriander leaves

2 limes, cut into wedges

Hot & sour eggplant

125ml light-flavoured oil, for frying

4 baby eggplants (aubergines), thickly sliced

100ml tamari

100ml mirin

50ml rice vinegar

1 tablespoon agave syrup

1 small chilli, finely sliced

4cm piece fresh ginger, peeled and sliced into matchsticks

2 spring onions, finely sliced

This is my variation on the classic miso-marinated cod from the wonderful Nobu restaurants, plus an attempt to make (my favourite) eggplant more interesting for my family. You could serve this with some rice, but the salmon and eggplant are actually rich and filling without any other accompaniment, making this a fantastic carb-free meal if you're into that.

To make the marinade, mix the sugar, mirin and sake together in a small pan and bring to the boil. Reduce the heat to a gentle simmer for 2–3 minutes, stirring until the sugar has dissolved. Take off the heat and whisk in the miso. Stir in the chilli bean paste and leave to cool.

Put the salmon in a non-reactive dish, cover with the marinade, cover the dish and refrigerate overnight.

To make the hot & sour eggplant, heat the oil in a large frying pan over medium heat. Shallow-fry the eggplant in batches of 4–5 slices, turning after 1 minute, until golden on all sides. Drain on kitchen paper while you cook the rest.

To make the soy mirin dressing, whisk together the tamari, mirin, rice vinegar and agave in a large bowl. Whisk in the chilli, ginger and spring onion. Add the eggplant and toss gently to coat.

Cook the edamame according to the packet instructions, and drain.

Remove the salmon from the marinade. Heat a large frying pan over medium–high heat and cook the salmon for 6–8 minutes, turning once, or until cooked to your liking.

Serve the eggplant and salmon sprinkled with edamame, pea shoots and coriander, with lime wedges on the side.

Seared bream & braised white beans with green olive & citrus salsa

Serves 4

Braised white beans

5 garlic cloves, roughly chopped
1 white onion, thinly sliced
2 x 400g tins cannellini beans, rinsed
2 bay leaves
500ml vegetable stock
100ml extra virgin olive oil

Green olive & citrus salsa

200g green olives, pitted and roughly chopped
Zest of 1 lemon
1 garlic clove, finely chopped
1 spring onion, finely chopped
1 handful coriander leaves, chopped
50ml extra virgin olive oil

4 bream fillets
1 tablespoon olive oil
1 lemon, cut into wedges, to serve

We all now know the health benefits of the olive oil, fish and vegetable-rich Mediterranean diet; our strong Italian and Greek communities in Australia have been quietly teaching us to eat that way for years. The white beans make a delicious change from potato and if you use pitted olives for the salsa there's barely anything to do here.

To make the braised white beans, put the garlic, onion, beans, bay leaves and stock in a large pan and simmer over medium heat for 20–25 minutes, until the onions and garlic are soft. Stir in the olive oil and season to taste.

Meanwhile, to make the salsa, mix together all the ingredients and season to taste.

Season the bream with salt. Heat the olive oil in a frying pan over high heat and add the fish, skin side down. Reduce the heat to medium and cook the fish for 4–5 minutes or until almost cooked. Turn the fish, remove the pan from the heat and leave the fish to finish cooking in the heat of the pan for a further 2 minutes.

Serve the bream with the braised beans and salsa, and lemon wedges for squeezing.

Roast chicken & fennel with buckwheat & parsley salad

Serves 4

2 fennel bulbs, sliced
1 large onion, cut into thick wedges
1 pinch saffron strands
150ml chicken stock
4 chicken Marylands (leg and thigh)
½ teaspoon crushed chilli flakes
Olive oil, to drizzle
Rind from ½ preserved lemon, chopped
100g green olives

Buckwheat & parsley salad

80g buckwheat
100g quinoa
500ml vegetable stock
Seeds from 1 pomegranate
1 large bunch parsley, chopped
1 small handful mint, chopped
1 large bunch coriander, chopped
100ml olive oil
Zest and juice of 1 lemon
100g toasted almonds, crushed

Green harissa

1 large handful parsley
1 large bunch coriander
1 green chilli
1 garlic clove
4 tablespoons olive oil, plus extra
if needed

With its rich Middle-Eastern flavours, this plate is rather tagine like; the addition of the buckwheat salad and harissa complete the setting. You could grate a little chorizo over the top of the roast chicken if you liked.

Preheat the oven to 200°C. Place the fennel bulbs and onion in a large roasting tin. Scatter with the saffron and pour in the chicken stock.

Rub the chicken with chilli flakes and sea salt and arrange in the tin on top of the vegetables. Drizzle with olive oil and roast for 30–35 minutes until the chicken is golden. Scatter with the preserved lemon and olives, drizzle with more oil and roast for another 10–15 minutes.

Meanwhile, to make the buckwheat & parsley salad, put the buckwheat and quinoa in a large saucepan with the stock. Bring to the boil over high heat. Reduce the heat to medium–low and leave undisturbed for 15 minutes. Fluff with a fork, transfer to a bowl and leave to cool. Stir in the remaining ingredients.

To make the green harissa, blend all the ingredients together until smooth, adding more oil if necessary. Season to taste.

Serve the chicken and fennel with the buckwheat & parsley salad and green harissa.

Masala snapper with cumin-roast tomatoes

Serves 4

3 tablespoons olive oil

2 teaspoons ground turmeric

2 teaspoons masala powder

1 tablespoon ground cumin

4 x plate-sized snapper (about 600g) or 200g snapper fillets

Light-flavoured oil, for frying

1 bunch watercress

1 tablespoon extra virgin olive oil

2 apples, sliced very thinly (use a mandoline if you have one)

Cumin-roast tomatoes

500g heritage tomatoes, including cherry tomatoes

1 teaspoon cumin seeds

1 tablespoon chopped thyme leaves

2 tablespoons olive oil

Chilli & cumin dressing

2 teaspoons cumin seeds, toasted

2 red chillies, deseeded and chopped

½ teaspoon salt

2 teaspoons runny honey

3 tablespoons lime juice

A few years ago, Portugal exploded into the world of fashionably Instagrammable destinations. Living in London, I got caught up in the frenzy and we have had a couple of great holidays there. I love summer holiday cooking — just grilled fish and salad, day after day — and I would race off to the fish market every morning. Everything about it reminded me so much of Australia — except, my Portuguese is sadly not up to scratch and I was lucky to be able to buy anything. After a few visits, the fishermen realised they weren't going to get rid of me and took pity, opening up my whole fish from tip to tail, straight through the head. It was a revelation, and perfect for this recipe, but fillets will work well if that's what you have to hand.

Mix together the olive oil, turmeric, masala and cumin in a large bowl. Add the fish and leave to marinate for 1 hour.

Meanwhile, to make the cumin-roast tomatoes, preheat the oven to 200°C. Cut any larger tomatoes in half, leaving the cherry tomatoes whole. Place in a large roasting tin with the cumin seeds, thyme and oil. Season with salt and pepper and toss together well. Roast for about 30 minutes, until just starting to soften, then leave to cool.

To make the chilli & cumin dressing, pound the cumin, chilli and salt with a mortar and pestle. Add one of the cumin-roasted tomato halves and pound well. Stir in the honey and lime juice until well combined.

Lift the fish out of the marinade and season with salt. Heat 1 tablespoon oil in a frying pan over high heat. Add the fish, skin side down, reduce the heat to medium and cook for 4–5 minutes, or until almost cooked. Turn and cook on the other side for 1 minute.

Toss the watercress with extra virgin olive oil and season with salt. Serve the tomatoes with the fish, watercress and apple slices. Drizzle the dressing over the fish.

Seared duck breast with beetroot & cherry ponzu sauce

Serves 4

4 duck breasts, with skin

4 candy beets or other beetroot, steamed until tender, peeled and cut into eighths

1 bunch (about 360g) spring green leaves, rainbow chard or collard greens, blanched

80g cherries, halved and pitted

120ml mirin

80ml ponzu sauce (citrus soy)

This is a sort of updated eighties duck a l'orange — with the sweetness of the Australian cherries and a nod to Japan with that sour–tangy ponzu sauce. Duck might sound rather exotic — perhaps a 'restaurant meal' — but duck breasts are very simple to cook at home and deliciously impressive if you're having people for dinner. I usually cook everything fast, but here it's worth taking a bit of time to render the fat from the duck skin in the pan first, then you can pop it in the oven to cook through.

Preheat the oven to 200°C. Season the duck well and place, skin side down, in a cold ovenproof frying pan. Cook over medium–high heat until the fat is rendered and the skin browned. Turn the duck over and add the beetroot. Sear the other side of the duck and colour the beetroots, then transfer the pan to the oven for 4–5 minutes. Remove the duck and beetroot to plates to keep warm.

Colour the green leaves in the hot pan over medium heat on the stovetop, then remove to a plate.

Add the cherries to the pan, then add the mirin and ponzu and stir to deglaze the pan. Cook until the liquid has slightly reduced and thickened. Season to taste.

Carve the duck breasts into thick slices. Arrange the beetroot and greens around the duck and finish with the cherry ponzu sauce.

Five-spice braised beef with creamed sweet potato, chilli snake beans & impatient pickled herbs

Serves 4

Five-spice braised beef

800g beef shin, butterflied

Light-flavoured oil

2 litres chicken stock

2 lemongrass stalks, white part only, bruised and roughly chopped

200g fresh ginger, peeled and roughly chopped

1 whole garlic bulb, cloves separated, peeled and bruised

2 star anise

1 cinnamon stick, broken

60g palm sugar, crumbled or grated

1 heaped tablespoon tamarind purée

2 tablespoons fish sauce

Impatient pickled herbs

1 tablespoon mustard seeds

100ml rice wine vinegar

80g icing sugar

1 teaspoon salt

1 handful coriander leaves

1 red chilli, very finely sliced

2 spring onions, finely sliced

Creamed sweet potato

400g sweet potatoes, peeled and cut into chunks

125ml cream

30g butter

Chilli snake beans

320g snake beans or green beans, topped and tailed

4 tablespoons garlic chilli paste

1 tablespoon olive oil

I'm serving this as a dinner plate, but it's actually based on a Vietnamese breakfast dish — the beef is slow braised with carrots, then shredded and served in a baguette with hot mint, coriander and Thai basil. So, if you have any leftover braised beef, you know what to do with it. The pickling method used here for the herbs is perfect for the impatient cook.

To braise the beef, lightly rub the beef with oil and season well. Put the beef in a large heavy-based pan over medium–high heat. Sear for 6 minutes, turning once.

Add the remaining ingredients to the pan with the beef. Reduce the heat to low–medium, cover the pan and leave to braise for 4 hours or until the beef is tender. Remove from the heat and leave the beef to cool in the braising liquid.

To make the impatient pickled herbs, warm the mustard seeds in a saucepan over medium heat until they start to pop. Add the vinegar, sugar and salt and 200ml water and warm gently until the sugar and salt have dissolved. Remove from the heat and allow to cool, then pour over the coriander, chilli and spring onions and toss together. Use immediately or leave to pickle for a while.

Meanwhile, cook the sweet potato in a large pan of simmering water for 15–20 minutes until tender. Drain and return to the hot pan. Mash, add the cream and butter and beat with a wooden spoon until smooth. Season well.

To make the chilli snake beans, blanch the beans in boiling water for a couple of minutes until just tender. Drain and return to the hot pan. Add the garlic chilli paste and olive oil and toss over medium heat for 2 minutes to warm through.

Lift the cooled beef from the pan and strain the braising liquid into a fresh pan over medium heat, discarding the vegetables and spices. Return the beef to the strained liquid, gently breaking it apart. Warm the beef and liquid gently.

Serve the beef and chilli snake beans with creamed sweet potato and the braising liquid spooned over the top. Top with the impatient pickled herbs.

Parmesan-crumbed chicken schnitzel with creamed corn & heritage tomato salad

Serves 4

4 chicken escalopes
75g plain flour
2 tablespoons milk
1 egg
30g fresh breadcrumbs
45g grated parmesan
3 tablespoons chopped parsley
1 tablespoon chopped thyme
½ teaspoon salt
3 tablespoons olive oil
1 lemon wedges, cut into wedges, to serve

Creamed corn

50g butter
200g red onion, finely sliced
1 garlic clove, sliced
2 teaspoons sliced red chilli
250g sweetcorn, cut from the cob
50ml double cream

Heritage tomato salad

2 tomatoes, cut into wedges
2 green tomatoes, cut into wedges
1 red onion, finely sliced
1 bunch parsley
1 tablespoon ground sumac
120ml olive oil

Along with the meat pie, this has to be Australia's favourite pub food. We see a really good schnitty as one of our basic human rights. This is the comfort food of my childhood, updated with a heritage tomato salad. This schnitty first appeared in Sydney Food, *with creamed potato and a crisp fennel salad – it was on our first dinner menu when we opened bills Surry Hills, and it's been there ever since.*

Place the escalopes between sheets of baking paper on a board and flatten by gently hitting with a rolling pin.

Place the flour in a shallow bowl. Lightly beat the milk and egg in another bowl. Mix together the breadcrumbs, parmesan, parsley, thyme, salt and pepper in a third bowl.

Dip each chicken escalope in the flour, then the egg, then in the breadcrumbs, shaking off the excess.

Heat the oil in a large frying pan over medium heat. Add the chicken (you might need to cook in batches to avoid overcrowding) and cook for 2 minutes on each side or until golden brown. Drain on kitchen paper.

Meanwhile, to make the creamed corn, heat the butter in a saucepan until sizzling. Add the onion, garlic and chilli. Cook until the onion is translucent. Add the sweetcorn, cover the pan and simmer gently for 20 minutes or until tender. Add the cream and 50ml water and bring to a simmer. Remove one-third of the corn from the pan and blend until smooth. Return the blended corn to the saucepan and mix through. Season well and set aside to cool.

For the heritage tomato salad, toss together the tomatoes, onion and parsley with the sumac. Toss with the olive oil and a sprinkling of salt.

Serve the schnitzels with the creamed corn and tomato salad, with lemon wedges on the side.

Sweet

Pavlova with mango, passionfruit & yoghurt cream

Serves 8

Pavlova

6 large egg whites
200g caster sugar
150g soft brown sugar
2 teaspoons lemon juice

Yoghurt cream

500ml double cream
150g Greek yoghurt

To serve

2 mangoes, sliced
Pulp of 4 passionfruit
Lime zest or chopped pistachio nuts

When we were first opening in Japan, we had a pop-up café for a weekend. There was to be a big press launch on the first day and we had painstakingly prepared our menu, including true Aussie pavlovas. Then we discovered the only oven in the café was a pizza oven. Pavlova in a pizza oven is quite a challenge — we were up until 2am, but the team pulled it out of a hat and everyone went crazy for the pav.

You can fold a handful of chopped pistachios or chocolate chips into the meringue, depending on the season. I love the slight sourness of the yoghurt cream that prevents this whole dish self-combusting into a sugar rush.

To make the pavlova, preheat the oven to 160°C. Line 2 large baking trays with baking paper.

Whisk the egg whites and a pinch of salt with electric beaters until soft peaks form. Mix the sugars together. With the beaters running, gradually add the sugar a spoonful at a time, beating until dissolved after each addition. Beat until all the sugar has been added and the mixture forms glossy stiff peaks. Beat in the lemon juice.

Use a large metal spoon to spoon 8 large even mounds of meringue onto the baking trays, leaving room for spreading. Make an indent in the centre of each.

Reduce the oven to 110°C. Place the meringues in the oven and cook for 1 hour 30 minutes. Switch off the oven, open the door slightly and leave the meringues to cool completely in the oven.

For the yoghurt cream, beat the cream and yoghurt together briefly until thick.

Crack a hole in the top of each pavlova, spoon the yoghurt cream over the top and add sliced mango and passionfruit pulp. Scatter with lime zest or chopped pistachios to serve.

Lemon zabaglione with summer berries

Serves 6

Lemon zabaglione

3 egg yolks
100g demerara sugar
Zest and juice of 1 lemon
150g crème fraiche

To serve

600g mixed berries (strawberries,
raspberries, blueberries, red currants
or blackberries)
40g crushed amaretti biscuits

*There are Italian restaurants in Melbourne that
have been there since before I was born. They
are woven into the fabric of our life in Australia.
This simple creamy dessert of citrus flavours
will forever remind me of being invited to lunch
by a magazine editor in the early nineties,
when the expense accounts were heady and the
weekend started at noon on a Friday. She entirely
disregarded the fabulous menu, coolly ordering
grilled fish and undressed leaves instead. I was
anxious that this signalled the dessert trolley would
be waved away. I need not have fretted: it seems the
plain fish was her trade-off to enjoying expense-
account zabaglione several times a week.*

To make the lemon zabaglione, place the egg yolks, sugar,
lemon zest and juice in a stainless steel bowl over a pan of
simmering water. Use electric beaters to beat for about
5 minutes, until pale, thick and creamy.

Transfer to another bowl to cool, stirring occasionally to
release the heat, then stir in the crème fraiche.

Serve the lemon zabaglione and berries, sprinkled with
the crushed amaretti.

Chocolate sorbet with macerated cherries, chocolate crumb & almond brittle

Serves 8

Chocolate sorbet

200g caster sugar
75g Dutch cocoa
1 teaspoon vanilla bean extract
180g dark (70%) chocolate, broken into small pieces
2 tablespoons vodka, optional

Macerated cherries

300g cherries, halved and pitted
100g sugar
50ml maraschino cherry syrup
50ml crème de cassis

Chocolate crumb

100g caster sugar
70g dark chocolate, chopped

Almond brittle

125g sugar
25g flaked almonds

This is a very intense hit of chocolatiness. Leave out the vodka, if you prefer, but it helps prevent ice crystals in the sorbet. Even if you cheat here and buy the sorbet — and you'll never be frowned on for time-saving short cuts in an Australian kitchen — it's still a pretty easy show-stopping dessert, showcasing our favourite summer cherries.

To make the chocolate sorbet, stir together the sugar, cocoa, vanilla and a pinch of salt in a large saucepan with 500ml water. Bring to the boil, whisking occasionally, and then whisk continuously while it boils for 60 seconds. Remove from the heat and add the chocolate, whisking until melted. Whisk in the vodka. Allow to cool, then churn in an ice-cream maker, according to the manufacturer's instructions. If you don't have an ice-cream maker, pour into a loaf tin and place in the freezer for 8 hours, breaking up with a fork every couple of hours until frozen.

To make the macerated cherries, put the cherries in a bowl. Put the sugar, cherry syrup and crème de cassis in a pan with 50ml water, bring to the boil and then simmer until reduced and syrupy. Pour over the cherries and leave to steep for at least 1 hour. Store in the fridge in an airtight container until ready to serve.

To make the chocolate crumb, heat the sugar in a pan with 2 tablespoons water. Once the sugar has fully dissolved and turned golden brown, add the chocolate and remove from the heat. Stir continuously until the mixture forms into crumbs. Store in an airtight container until ready to serve.

To make the almond brittle, place the sugar in a heavy-based pan with 25ml water and heat gently. When the mixture is starting to turn golden brown, stir in the almonds. Cook until deep caramel in colour and then pour onto a sheet of greased baking paper. Place another piece of greased paper on top and roll the caramel out thinly. Leave to cool completely, break into shards and store in an airtight container for up to 5 days.

Serve the sorbet with the macerated cherries, chocolate crumb and shards of almond brittle.

Hazelnut & caramel cakes
with mascarpone cream

Serves 10

Hazelnut & caramel cakes

400ml tin condensed milk, unopened
Melted butter and plain flour, to coat
250g butter, chopped
250g soft brown sugar
4 eggs
125g ground toasted hazelnuts, plus
extra toasted hazelnuts, to serve
125g plain flour
1 teaspoon baking powder

Mascarpone cream

100g mascarpone
100ml double cream
40g icing sugar
½ teaspoon vanilla bean paste

Caramel has certainly been enjoying a decade in the sun. These little cakes are like mini fondant desserts; serve them warm so that when you cut into them the caramel oozes out.

To make the cakes, place the unopened tin of condensed milk in a large saucepan and fill with water. Make sure the tin is completely submerged and covered by about 3cm of water. Cover, bring to a simmer, then tilt the pan lid slightly and simmer for 3 hours, topping up with boiling water to keep the tin covered. Remove from the heat and leave to cool. Open the tin and scoop the caramel into a bowl.

Preheat the oven to 200°C. Brush ten 160ml dariole moulds with melted butter, then add a little flour and tilt to coat evenly. Shake out the excess.

Cream together the butter and sugar until light and fluffy. Beat the eggs in one by one. Gently fold in the ground hazelnuts, flour and baking powder.

Fill the moulds halfway with cake mixture, then make a little indent and spoon in a tablespoon of caramel (you won't use it all up). Spoon more cake mixture into the moulds to cover the caramel. You should have about 1cm space at the top of each mould for the cake to rise. Give the mould a tap to settle the mixture. Bake for 15 minutes, then leave for 5 minutes.

For the mascarpone cream, whisk all the ingredients together until thick.

Serve the cakes with mascarpone cream and a sprinkling of toasted hazelnuts.

Tip

Serve any leftover caramel as a topping for ice cream. Uncooked cakes can be refrigerated in an airtight container for up to 3 days. Return to room temperature before baking. The mascarpone cream will keep in the fridge for 1 day.

Black sticky rice with coconut milk & papaya

Serves 4

300g Thai black sticky rice
1 pandan leaf
110g caster sugar
250ml coconut milk, plus extra to serve
Papaya, chopped, to serve
Zest and juice of 1 lime, to serve

This visually stunning Asian rice pudding has been a favourite in Australia for decades, and has made appearances on the menu at bills since we first opened. Pandan leaves are easily bought at Asian supermarkets these days. I first encountered them many years ago when a Nyonya friend baked a pandan chiffon cake. It was so exotic and new at the time — today it is so popular that you can buy packets of pandan lamingtons in the shops.

Rinse the rice under cold running water. Put the rice in a pan with 600ml water, the pandan leaf and a large pinch of salt. Bring to the boil and then cover with a tight-fitting lid. Reduce to a low simmer and cook for around 30 minutes. The rice is ready when it feels al dente.

Remove the pandan leaf and add the sugar and coconut milk to the rice. Stir over low heat until heated through and creamy. Serve in bowls with chunks of papaya, a drizzle of coconut milk, and lime zest and juice.

Tip

I find the cooking time of this rice can vary, depending on the brand you buy. If it's not cooked after 30 minutes, add a little more water and cook until done. Serve warm, cold or at room temperature.

Condensed milk semifreddo with jasmine-poached peaches

Serves 6

Condensed milk semifreddo

400ml condensed milk
380ml double cream
1 tablespoon vanilla bean paste
50ml maple syrup

Jasmine-poached peaches

300g sugar
2 tablespoons freeze-dried
strawberry powder
1 lemon, cut in half
1½ tablespoons jasmine tea leaves
4 peaches, each cut into 8 wedges,
pitted

To serve

100g raspberries
45g roasted pistachios, crushed

This is all about the semifreddo – the peaches are in the bowl just to give it a vaguely healthy spin! Condensed milk is something I drank straight from the tin as a child – then the world got even brighter and it was packaged into tubes that I could sneak out of the fridge and suck when my mother wasn't looking. Make a big batch of this semifreddo, keep it in the freezer and impress your friends by using it to make the best-ever affogato. (Affogato is a marvellous dinner party trick – have tiny individual bowls of ice cream in the freezer ready to go, then simply pour the coffee over.)

To make the semifreddo, whisk together all the ingredients to thick peaks with an electric mixer. Spoon into an airtight container and freeze for at least 4 hours and up to 2 weeks.

For the poached peaches, stir together the sugar, strawberry powder and 500ml water in a large saucepan. Squeeze in the juice from the lemon and add the squeezed lemon halves to the pan too. Add the jasmine tea leaves. Bring to a simmer over medium–low heat and cook for 15 minutes. Strain the mixture through a fine sieve and return to the pan.

Add the peaches to the pan and simmer for 6–8 minutes until just tender. Using a slotted spoon, transfer the peaches to an airtight container. Return the pan to high heat and cook the liquid for 5 minutes or until reduced by half. Pour over the peaches and leave to cool. Cover and refrigerate for up to 2 days.

To serve, lightly crush the raspberries with half the peach syrup and spoon into bowls. Pour the remaining syrup over the top, then add a ball of semifreddo and some peach wedges. Sprinkle with crushed pistachios.

Tip

If you can't find the powder, buy freeze-dried whole strawberries at large greengrocers and grind them down.

Pink grapefruit crème caramels
with grapefruit & raspberry granita

Serves 8

Grapefruit & raspberry granita

150g flesh from 2 large pink grapefruit, cut into segments, membrane removed
50ml pink grapefruit juice
40g sugar
10g freeze-dried raspberries

Pink grapefruit crème caramels

100g caster sugar
1 tablespoon pink grapefruit juice
270ml condensed milk
100ml double cream
400ml milk
3 eggs
1 teaspoon vanilla bean paste
1 teaspoon finely grated pink grapefruit zest
1 generous pinch sea salt flakes

To serve

160g fresh raspberries
50g crushed freeze-dried raspberries

Crème caramel, or 'flan', has been loved in France and Spain for centuries, but had its big restaurant heyday in the eighties. It is my absolute favourite comfort food dessert. I've added the bittersweet tang of grapefruit juice and a rose-pink raspberry granita that reminds me of cherry blossom. Stir a tablespoon of gin into the granita, for bite.

To make the granita, put the grapefruit flesh, juice, sugar, freeze-dried raspberries and 50ml water in a blender and mix until smooth. Pour into a shallow non-reactive container and freeze for about 1 hour, until starting to harden around the edges, then scrape into granules with a fork every 30 minutes for 4 hours. Transfer to an airtight container and keep frozen for up to 5 days.

For the crème caramels, preheat the oven to 160°C and grease eight 125ml ramekins.

Mix the sugar with 20ml water in a heavy-based saucepan. Place over low heat until the sugar dissolves and turns golden brown. Carefully (it will spit) add the grapefruit juice and swirl the pan to mix. Pour into the ramekins and place the ramekins in a large deep roasting tin.

Whisk together the condensed milk, cream, milk, eggs, vanilla, grapefruit zest and salt and pour into the ramekins. Pour enough boiling water into the roasting tin to come halfway up the sides of the ramekins. Bake for 30 minutes, or until the crème caramels are set, but with a wobble.

Remove the ramekins and leave to cool slightly, then refrigerate for at least 2 hours and up to 2 days.

To serve, dip the bases of the ramekins into hot water (if you have refrigerated overnight, you might not need to do this). Dry the bases (to avoid drips), then turn out onto plates, running a knife around the edge to loosen if necessary.

Serve the crème caramels with the granita and fresh and freeze-dried raspberries.

Honey & tahini semifreddo with gin-soaked blackberries

Serves 4—6

Honey & tahini semifreddo

8 egg yolks
100g caster sugar
110g tahini
300ml single cream
85g runny honey

Gin-soaked blackberries

50g caster sugar
50ml gin
200g frozen blackberries
Juice of ½ lime

Sesame & cacao nib snap

100g caster sugar
20g butter
35g sesame seeds, toasted
20g cacao nibs

Gin has certainly enjoyed a makeover in recent years, with small boutique producers and added botanicals giving it a whole new sophisticated lease of life — a far cry from Hogarth's Gin Lane. Its slight bitterness makes it ideal for soaking sweet fruit and pairing with a creamy semifreddo.

The quantity of semifreddo here will serve 12, so you could halve it if you like, but it's easy enough to make a good batch to keep in the freezer.

To make the semifreddo, use electric beaters to beat the egg yolks and sugar until light and fluffy, then whisk in the tahini until smooth. Whip the cream and honey to soft peaks in another bowl and then slowly combine the two mixtures. Pour into an airtight container and freeze for several hours.

To make the gin-soaked blackberries, stir together the sugar, gin and 50ml water in a pan over medium heat. Bring to the boil, reduce the heat and simmer until syrupy. Add the blackberries and squeeze in the lime juice. Cool and store in an airtight container in the fridge for up to 2 weeks.

To make the sesame and cacao nib snap, line a large baking tray with foil. Place the sugar in a heavy-based frying pan over medium heat and cook until lightly golden and almost all dissolved. Add the butter and swirl the pan to combine. Cook for a further minute or so, until golden brown. Stir in the sesame seeds and cacao nibs, pour onto the foil and spread to about 3mm thick. Leave for about 20 minutes to cool and set.

To serve, crumble the sesame and cacao nib snap into shallow bowls. Top with a scoop of semifreddo and the gin-soaked blackberries.

Rhubarb & lime crumble with crème anglaise

Serves 8

1kg rhubarb, cut into 5cm lengths
Zest and juice of 1 orange
2 makrut lime leaves
15g fresh ginger, peeled and finely grated
200g soft brown sugar
115g plain flour
115g chilled butter, diced
100g rolled oats
1 handful macadamia nuts, chopped

Vanilla crème anglaise

250ml milk
200ml single cream
1 vanilla bean, split, seeds scraped
3 egg yolks
75g caster sugar

The fresh makrut lime leaves add an unexpected perfumed twist to this classic recipe. You can buy them now in supermarkets (they used to be called kaffir limes), but if you have trouble finding them, use the zest of a regular lime instead. I don't advise using the dried lime leaves sold in the spice section.

Preheat the oven to 200°C. Put the rhubarb, orange zest and juice, lime leaves, ginger and half the sugar into an ovenproof dish. Stir well and then bake for 20 minutes, until the rhubarb has started to soften.

Place the remaining sugar, flour and butter in a bowl and rub between your fingertips until it resembles breadcrumbs. Stir in the oats and nuts and scatter over the rhubarb, pushing the topping down into the fruit. Bake for 25 minutes.

For the vanilla crème anglaise, stir together the milk, cream, vanilla bean and seeds in a small saucepan over medium–low heat and bring just to the boil.

Whisk the egg yolks and sugar in a heatproof bowl until pale and creamy. Slowly add the hot milk, whisking constantly. Wash and dry the saucepan and then pour the custard back into the pan. Stir over low heat for about 5 minutes, until just thickening enough to coat the back of a spoon – but don't let it boil. Can be served hot, just warm or even cold, with the rhubarb crumble.

Pineapple tarte Tatin with toasted coconut sorbet

Serves 10

Toasted coconut sorbet

25g shredded coconut
400ml coconut cream
250ml coconut milk
200g caster sugar

Pineapple tarte Tatin

1 fresh pineapple
100g butter
355g caster sugar
700g ready-rolled frozen puff pastry, just thawed

To serve

Toasted coconut
Zest and juice of 1 lime

The French make tarte Tatin in their impeccably fine-dining fashion, with carefully layered and interwoven wafer-thin slices of apple. This is our laid-back Aussie version — the rings of fresh pineapple in a sticky caramel work a dream.

To make the sorbet, place the coconut in a dry frying pan and stir over medium heat for 2–3 minutes until golden. Transfer to a saucepan, add the coconut cream, milk and sugar and stir over medium heat until the sugar dissolves.

Pour into a heatproof bowl and leave to cool, stirring occasionally to release the heat. Place in the fridge for at least 6 hours, or overnight, until well chilled. Churn in an ice-cream machine according to the manufacturer's instructions, then spoon into an airtight container and freeze overnight until firm.

To make the pineapple tarte Tatin, preheat the oven to 200°C. Peel, core and cut the pineapple into 2.5cm thick slices.

Melt the butter in a heavy-based, non-stick frying pan. Add the sugar and cook until it dissolves and turns dark caramel. Shake the pan gently as it cooks to prevent the caramel catching and burning.

Pour the caramel into a shallow 25 x 38cm baking tray so that it evenly covers the base. Lay the pineapple slices on top of the caramel in a single layer.

Roll out the puff pastry to 27 x 40cm (just larger than your baking tray) and lay it over the pineapple and caramel, tucking in the edges (take care as the caramel will be hot).

Bake in the oven for 18–20 minutes, until the pastry is puffed and golden. Leave to cool slightly before turning out onto a large board or platter and cutting into squares.

Sprinkle with a little coconut and lime zest and serve with toasted coconut sorbet.

Mango & lime meringue pie

Serves 8

Pastry

225g plain flour
125g chilled butter, diced
2 tablespoons iced water

Mango & lime filling

350g mango purée (around 3 large
mangoes, or use thawed frozen fruit)
60ml lime juice
2 teaspoons finely grated lime zest
4 egg yolks
100g caster sugar
60g cold butter, diced
5g gelatine leaves

Meringue

200g caster sugar
4 egg whites

*When we photographed this, I commented that
in the restaurants we use a blowtorch to get that
golden meringue. I'd been living in London and the
food stylist in New York and we both said 'but no
one will have a blowtorch at home'. The Aussies
in the kitchen were aghast: 'Of course they will.
After MasterChef, everyone owns a blowtorch.'
We Aussies take our food very seriously. If you're
not such a keen blowtorcher, toast this under a
superhot grill for a minute instead.*

To make the pastry, pulse the flour and butter in a food
processor until it resembles breadcrumbs. Add the water
and pulse again until it starts to clump together. Don't
overprocess or the pastry will be tough. Gather into a ball
and roll out on baking paper to fit a 23cm wide, 3cm deep
springform tin. Ease into the tin and chill for 20 minutes.

Meanwhile, preheat the oven to 180°C. Line the pastry with
baking paper and pastry weights or uncooked rice or beans.
Blind bake for 15 minutes, then remove the paper and
weights and bake for 10 minutes until golden and dry. Cool.

For the filling, stir the mango, lime juice and zest in a pan
over medium heat until hot. Meanwhile, whisk the egg yolks
and sugar in a heatproof bowl until pale and creamy. Slowly
add the hot mango to the bowl, whisking constantly. Pour
back into the pan and stir over low heat for about 5 minutes,
until the mixture thickens, but don't let it boil. Whisk in the
butter, a few pieces at a time.

Soak the gelatine in cold water for 5 minutes, until soft.
Squeeze out the water and stir the gelatine into the filling.
Cool, pour into the pastry and chill for 1 hour, or until set.

For the meringue, stir the sugar and 125ml water in a small
pan over low heat, without boiling, until dissolved. Increase
the heat and bring to the boil. Cook until the syrup reaches
hard ball stage (121°C on a thermometer). Meanwhile, beat
the egg whites until soft peaks form. Slowly pour the hot
syrup onto the egg white, beating continuously. Keep beating
for 5 minutes until thick, glossy and cooled. Spoon over the
filling and swirl to create peaks. Use a blowtorch or very hot
grill to lightly brown the meringue.

Thank you

I'm often asked how I run restaurants around the world. Of course, it's not just about me. Over nearly 30 years I've worked with an incredible array of talented, wonderful people, so a big thank you to everyone who has helped me to keep cooking and serving those (ricotta) hotcakes.

To the team now: Avron, Toby and Toby, for looking after the day-to-day so that I can continue be creative, and flippant, and ridiculous, and impetuous, and loving, and enthusiastic; Caroline for driving the creative process through to RESULTS with diplomacy, humour and charm; and Louis, for the constant inspiration, passion and warmth. I'd like to also thank Mina, Norihito, Tarumi-san and Nakamura-san for taking us on a big Japanese, Korean and Hawaiian adventure that has made me lucky enough to think of Japan as my third home.

Another joy of being in business for so long is the many deep long-term relationships I get to enjoy and be influenced and nurtured by. To Bruce and Jules, who make our restaurants more like my home, and keep me inspired every day – a creative repartee I couldn't do without, it's like my lifeblood, To Mary, for extending what we do in the restaurants to print and type and communication, and for keeping us on the straight and narrow so that it all makes sense together. To Clare Lattin and Maria Farmer, who forever have helped us with our exchanges with the world outside ours. Thank you to Lauren, Stephanie and Vince for keeping the accounts ship-shape and therefore able to weather the long term (and perhaps even a global pandemic). To Will and Jonny, for believing in Natalie and me in the early days in the UK, and never missing a board meeting since. To Peter, for your sage and wise advice and help, and for being the best at budgets and teaching all of us the beauty in them.

To Jane M and Lou, for convincing me that I had another book in me. To Jane P, for the irreverent musings on life and my words. To Frith, for helping me capture what it means to me to be Australian in the book design, and for taking me on a revelatory creative journey. To Mikkel and Susie, for their irrepressible energy and for making the last shot feel like the first, and to Wilson and his team, and the team from bills in Sydney, for getting the food on the plate for the shoot – it takes many hands.

Australian food has taken some exciting leaps in all kinds of directions and I wait with bated breath to see where it goes next. So many of my peers have developed and conjured up all manner of expressions that thrill and excite and entice and make our lives all the more interesting for their creations.

A few of the recipes in this book are meals from home, but most are dishes that have appeared on our menus over the last 27 years. They are created with our chefs and customer feedback and local inspiration. Favourite recipes become a personal biography, reminding you of life's markers with a flavour on the tongue or a cooking aroma. I hope you enjoy cooking and eating these as much as I have.

And to Natalie, Edie, Inès and Bunny for humouring me and loving me, and appreciating everything I cook – even if Inès can do it better.

Index

Published in 2020 by Murdoch Books, an imprint of Allen & Unwin

Murdoch Books Australia
83 Alexander Street, Crows Nest NSW 2065
Phone: +61 (0)2 8425 0100
murdochbooks.com.au
info@murdochbooks.com.au

Murdoch Books UK
Ormond House, 26–27 Boswell Street,
London, WC1N 3JZ
Phone: +44 (0) 20 8785 5995
murdochbooks.co.uk
info@murdochbooks.co.uk

For corporate orders & custom publishing contact our business
development team at salesenquiries@murdochbooks.com.au

Publisher: Jane Morrow
Editorial manager: Jane Price
Design concept and cover: Studio Frith, London
Illustrations: Studio Frith, London
Design manager: Megan Pigott
Layout designer: Sarah Odgers
Photography: Mikkel Vang
Photography assisted by: Klint Collier
Food and props stylist: Susie Theodorou
Props assisted by: Lauren Miller
Food preparation for photography: Wilson Chung; Hannah Wilmott; Jessica Godtschalk;
    Satoshi Yamamoto; Rick Duong; Kandi Liu; Lauren Danecek; Kat Hunt; Tammi Kwok
Food editors: Wilson Chung, Tracy Rutherford, Rosie Reynolds
Proofreader and indexer: Justine Harding
Production director: Lou Playfair

For Bill Granger
Producer: Natalie Elliott
Global project manager: Caroline Gladstone
Development chef: Louis Solley

Text © Bill Granger 2020
Design © Studio Frith 2020
Photography © Mikkel Vang 2020

ISBN 978 1 76052 598 9 Australia
ISBN 978 1 91163 296 2 UK

A cataloguing-in-publication entry
is available from the catalogue of
the National Library of Australia at
nla.gov.au

A catalogue record for this book is available from
the British Library

Colour reproduction by Splitting Image Colour
Studio Pty Ltd, Clayton, Victoria

Printed by C & C Offset Printing Co Ltd, China
10 9 8 7 6 5 4 3

Cooking temperatures given are for conventional
ovens. If you are using a fan-forced oven, please set
the temperature to 20 degrees lower.

The publisher and stylist would like to thank the
following for the generous loan of props for
photography: Mud Australia (mudaustralia.com);
Dinosaur designs (dinosaurdesigns.com); Szilvassy
ceramics available at Koskela (koskela.com.au);
Euro Marble (NSW) Pty Ltd (euromarble.com.au);
Meacham Nockles Design (meachamnockles.com)

The paper in this book is FSC® certified.
FSC® promotes environmentally
responsible, socially beneficial and
economically viable management of
the world's forests.